Pension at Stake

"There is a need to reform the defined benefit pension scheme. There will be longevity risk in the long run as the life expectancy of the pensioner increases, coupled with the issue of an ageing society and declining trend of fertility rate among the younger generation. It is important for the pension authority to prepare ahead in order to avoid any shock to the pension scheme. The authors have made a bold attempt to look into this pertinent issue."

—Hooy Chee Wooi, *Professor of Finance, School of Management, Universiti Sains Malaysia, President, Malaysian Finance Association*

"In this insightful examination of Malaysia's pension dynamics, the study becomes a powerful tool for social change, enhanced by the use of robust applied financial econometrics. It digs deep into the core issues, addressing not just financial complexities but the broader societal impact. The research bravely uncovers the flaws in the Malaysian civil service pension plan, offering potential remedies that could reshape the Malaysian welfare state. The study not only transcends numbers but provides a sophisticated understanding of assets and liabilities. An important read that brings attention to the human side of pension sustainability while recommending well-informed policies."

—Amri Rahamat, *Strategic Asset Allocation Professional*

"Embark on a journey into the future of Malaysian pensions with 'Navigating Longevity.' This book does not just offer solutions—it hands you a compass. Feel the critical pulse of pension sustainability for enduring financial resilience and security in the long run."

—Nidaa Ul-Husna Mazlan, *Risk Management Professional*

"*Pension at Stake* offers insightful analysis and viable solutions to the challenges faced by Malaysia's pension system - a must-read for financial professionals and policymakers."

—Ng Swee Kiang, *Head of Investment Education, Equities Tracker Holdings Berhad*

"As we navigate through the complexities of economic policy and financial management, grasping the detailed mechanics of pension systems like Malaysia's becomes not just beneficial but essential. This book does exactly that as it breaks down the multifaceted aspects of pension management, asset allocation and the looming concerns over long-term viability in a way that is both accessible and deeply informative. This book is a must-read for policymakers, financial professionals and anyone interested in the future of pension systems."

—Royce Tan, *Associate Director, MIDF Research*

Muhammad Irfan Abdul Rahman ·
Wee Yeap Lau

Pension at Stake

Issues and Solutions to Defined Benefit Pension Scheme in Malaysia

palgrave
macmillan

Muhammad Irfan Abdul Rahman
Faculty of Business and Economics
Universiti Malaya
Lembah Pantai, Kuala Lumpur
Malaysia

Wee Yeap Lau
Faculty of Business and Economics
Universiti Malaya
Lembah Pantai, Kuala Lumpur
Malaysia

ISBN 978-981-97-2323-2 ISBN 978-981-97-2324-9 (eBook)
https://doi.org/10.1007/978-981-97-2324-9

This Palgrave Macmillan imprint is published by the registered company Springer Nature Singapore Pte Ltd.
The registered company address is: 152 Beach Road, #21-01/04 Gateway East, Singapore 189721, Singapore

Paper in this product is recyclable.

Foreword

Pension funds, particularly for civil servants, have become a burning issue in light of Malaysia's tight fiscal space. In recent years, a raging debate has emerged over the rapidly rising operating expenditure, one that tends to overwhelm development expenditure and pose challenges given the flagging government revenue. Several obvious observations and questions come to mind: is the size of the civil service too large, and should the pension scheme be revised or even removed? Is the fiscal burden of huge pension payouts sustainable, with Malaysia's ageing population and higher longevity?

In 2024, it is expected that about 10.5% or RM32.4 billion of the federal government revenue will have to be used for retirement charges. It is worrisome that while the government expects a revenue of RM307.6 billion, federal government expenditure will be about RM393.8 billion, giving rise to a deficit of RM86.2 billion. It would be simplistic to think that this is the only figure that has to be considered. However, it certainly gives some flavour of the seriousness of the problem.

The existing fiscal situation forces us to draw attention to the existing pension scheme, which, indeed, must be reconsidered in view of the challenges it faces. The increasing longevity of the population and, therefore, of the fund's members pose a risk of its own, and it places pressures on the sustainability of the fund. Not only does the government have a heavier burden before it, but also those managing the fund have to ensure that the returns earned are acceptable. The management of the pension fund then becomes an issue at the micro-level quite, apart from the macro-pressures that have to be dealt with.

In view of the many questions that have to be answered, the state of pension funds in Malaysia is an important issue that demands attention. This book is a pertinent and timely contribution to the ongoing discussion, and it seriously addresses some of the problems that are troubling policymakers. This attempt is perhaps the first book-length treatment of the topic, with the authors undertaking a detailed empirical analysis based on which they have produced some recommendations. Anyone working on pension funds in Malaysia cannot afford to ignore this book.

Shankaran Nambiar
Head of Research, Malaysian
Institute of Economic Research
(MIER)
Kuala Lumpur, Malaysia

Preface

This book is conceived from a series of work done in the past three years. This book intends to examine a number of issues faced by the civil service pension scheme in Malaysia. As known by the public, the civil service pension scheme is administered by Kumpulan Wang Persaraan (Diperbadankan) (KWAP) or the Retirement Fund (Incorporated) that was established on 1 March 2007 under the Retirement Fund Act 2007 (Act 662), replacing the repealed Pensions Trust Fund Act 1991 (Act 454).

Increasing allocation under the fiscal budget under a decreasing fiscal space makes the issue of the government pension scheme a debatable issue. The Auditor General's Report published on October 10, 2023, revealed that federal liabilities were RM1.399 trillion at the end of 2022.

The federal liability ratio to gross domestic product (GDP) in 2022 was 78.1%, which has decreased as compared to 84.3% in 2021.

Against this backdrop, to quote some figures from the first MADANI 2023 budget, RM 39.5 billion is allocated to pension, retiring allowance, and gratuity, which is 11% more compared to the budget allocated in year 2022e (RM27.5 Billion). This allocation is expected to increase more, mainly due to the rising numbers of retirees, longer life expectancy and the salary increment during the service tenure. The increase in allocation to pensions is alarming, and some measures must be taken to control it.

A summary of the book: Chapter 1 briefly introduces the five pillars of pensions and Malaysia's pension scheme and provides an overview of the pension system in Malaysia. Chapter 2 examines the determinants of pension cost. It reviews previous literature on pension expenditure and provides some results to support the discussion. This study discusses the sustainability factors of pension obligations through pension-funded ratio, pension asset allocation investment, and pension-required return.

Chapter 3 focuses on the asset allocation in KWAP and how it impacts its return as investment income is one of the primary sources to sustain a pension scheme by KWAP's asset allocation. Chapter 4 reviews the long-term pension-funded status for KWAP in maintaining liabilities for the next ten years.

Chapter 5 intends to explore the required return for the Malaysia Retirement Fund to maintain an individual pension scheme. Scenario analysis has been implied based on four inputs of contribution rate, retirement age, life expectancy, and years of service in civil servants in calculating the required return. The applicability of longevity bonds in the Malaysian Capital Market is examined in Chapter 6.

Finally, the findings from all chapters are summarised in Chapter 7. The conclusion and recommendations for further research were discussed in this chapter. These findings are discussed in the context of implications for improving the defined benefit pension scheme.

Kuala Lumpur, Malaysia

Muhammad Irfan Abdul Rahman
Wee Yeap Lau

Contents

About the Authors

Muhammad Irfan Abdul Rahman is a Fund Manager at the RHB Asset Management Sdn Bhd and previously worked at Bank Simpanan Nasional, Central Bank of Malaysia and Bloomberg LP. He received his Ph.D. in Financial Economics and Master of Applied Statistics from the Faculty of Business and Economics, Universiti Malaya. He also received his bachelor's in Actuarial Science from the University of Nebraska Lincoln, USA.

Wee Yeap Lau is an Associate Professor at the Faculty of Business and Economics, Universiti Malaya, and previously served as Deputy Dean (Postgraduate) and Head of Department (Applied Statistics) of the Faculty of Economics and Administration. He is an Elected Member of the International Statistical Institute and an Executive Committee Member of the Malaysian Economic Association. He was a MEXT Scholar at Osaka University and a Visiting Scholar at the Risk Management Institute, National University of Singapore. He received his Ph.D. and Master in Economics from Osaka University. He also attended an Executive Education Program at Bendheim Center for Finance, Princeton University. He specialises in the economics of finance and investment.

Abbreviations

AFFB	Armed Forces Fund Board
CML	Capital Market Line
DB	Defined Benefit Pension Scheme
DC	Defined Contribution Pension Scheme
EPF	Employment Provident Fund
FBM KLCI	FTSE Bursa Malaysia Kuala Lumpur Composite Index
GNP	Gross National Product
KLCI	Kuala Lumpur Composite Index
KLSE	Kuala Lumpur Stock Exchange
KWAP	Retirement Fund Incorporated
KWSP	Kumpulan Wang Simpanan Pekerja
LTAT	Lembaga Tabung Angkatan Tentera
OPEX	Operating Expenditure
ROI	Return on Investment
RR	Required Rate of Return
SC	Securities Commission
SPV	Special Purpose Vehicle

List of Figures

List of Tables

CHAPTER 1

An Overview of the Pension System in Malaysia

1.1 Historical Development of Malaysia Civil Servant Pension

Historically, the Royal Suffian Commission for Public Services Officers endorsed the pension benefit implementation in 1968. Gratuity award (and derivative gratuity for the widow and children of a deceased officer) is acknowledged as the additional benefit on top of the pension/derivative pension. A derivative pension is given for 12.5 years from the retirement or death of a serving officer. After that, the Royal Harun Commission approved the pension benefit implementation for the personnel of statutory bodies and local authorities in May 1969. In January 1974, cash award in place of leave (GCR) was introduced at the rate of 1/30 last drawn salary for each day of leaves not utilised. In January 1976, the government agreed to provide a pension for the child of a deceased officer till the age of 21 or upon completing or ceasing to receive first-degree education at a higher learning institution, whichever applies as long the child is unmarried.

In October 1982, the government agreed to exempt any gratuity from the income tax. In January 2009, the minimum monthly pension was increased from RM280 to RM720. Even the derivative pension shall be paid 100% to the dependents. In April 1991, the period of service to qualify an employee for pensionable status was reduced from 10 to 3 years. In January 2004, the government agreed to grant a derivative

M. I. Abdul Rahman and W. Y. Lau, *Pension at Stake*,
https://doi.org/10.1007/978-981-97-2324-9_1

pension to the mother or father of an officer if he/she dies without leaving a spouse or children eligible for the derivative pension.

1.2 Pension Scheme and Five-Pillar Model

A pension scheme intends to give retirees and their surviving family members financial security in the event of retirement, death, or permanent disability. According to Holzmann and Hinz (2005), the importance of pension systems to a country's economic stability and the security of its elderly population has gained widespread acknowledgement during the past ten years. The World Bank (2008) created the five-pillar model, which describes the variety of design elements and provides a five-pillar model scheme to classify the various methods of funding the retirement system. The five-pillar framework of the World Bank (2008) is as illustrated below:

a. Zero Pillar (Non-Contributory): *"Basic" or "Social Pension" at the very least provides social aid, social protection for the elderly, and poverty protection.*
b. First Pillar (Mandatory): *Public pension plan, publicly managed, defined benefit, or nationally defined contributions. The goal is to prevent seniors from poverty and to stabilise their consumption.*
c. Second Pillar (Mandatory): *Typically refers to the individual savings account.*
d. Third Pillar (Voluntary): *Occupational or private pension programs, financed defined contribution or entirely or partially funded defined benefit.*
e. Fourth Pillar (Non-financial): *Access to formal social programmes, other informal social supports (such as family), and other private financial and non-financial resources.*

Regardless of the pillars, country-specific constraints necessitate executing a basic and carefully sequenced approach that will significantly narrow the range of viable possibilities. Each country must decide the specifics of its pension system, including any potential reforms. In Malaysia, the pension structure is composed of three main retirement schemes. The following are the primary pension plans as described by Malaysia's pension providers:

(i) Defined Contribution by Employee Provident Fund

The Employee Provident Fund (EPF) manages the Defined Contribution (DC) for non-pensionable civil officers and employees of the private sector. Under the DC retirement scheme, employees and employers regularly contribute monthly payments to the retirement fund.

(ii) Defined Benefit by Retirement Fund Incorporated (KWAP)

The Malaysian government offers the Defined Benefit (DB) pension programme for eligible civil personnel who meet the requirements. This civil service pension programme is a specific pension programme for public sector workers. The scheme is a government-sponsored retirement plan that provides benefits to employees such as monthly pensions and medical benefits. The Malaysia Pension Department calculates the benefits using a specified formula.

The plan guarantees life and adjusted payouts to account for inflation or the rising cost of living. The Malaysia Pension Department administers the Defined Benefit plan under the Ministry of Finance (MOF). Meanwhile, the Retirement Fund Incorporated (KWAP) serves as the appointed agent of the Federal government for pension fund collection and management (Retirement Fund Act, 2007).

This scheme also extends its benefit to the dependents of a deceased pensioner. This benefit is given to the dependents of a retiree who has passed away after retirement or while he/she is still working for the government. The pensionable officers are entitled to a service pension (a monthly payment), a service gratuity (a one-time payment), and financial rewards in place of leave (JPA, 2021).

(iii) Armed Forces Pension by the Armed Forces Fund Board (LTAT)

LTAT, a statutory organisation, handles the Malaysian Armed Forces' retirement fund, established in 1973 under the Armed Forces Fund Act (LTAT, 2022). However, the Ministry of Defense (MINDEF) is responsible for developing and reviewing its policies. At the same time, the Armed Forces Fund Board (LTAT) serves as an agent that operates the retirement fund.

Table 1.1 Overview of the pension provider in Malaysia

Category	*Armed forces*	*Pensionable civil service*	*Private sector and Non-pensionable civil service*
Policy Setting	Ministry of Defense (MINDEF)	Public Services Department (SPA)	EPF
Member Contribution Collection	Armed Forces Fund Board (LTAT)	KWAP	
Investment Policy & Guidelines			
Investment Management			
Benefit Payments and Admin	MINDEF		

Source KWAP Financial Report (2018), (KWAP, 2018)

The Defined Contribution scheme only depends on contributions and returns on assets accumulated by the fund. In contrast, the Defined Benefit scheme bases benefits entirely on the final salary and length of service (Barr & Diamond, 2006). Aside from these two pension schemes, the armed forces have the same pension structure as the Defined Contribution scheme by EPF.

The Malaysian pension scheme can be summarised as follows in Table 1.1.

1.3 Pension System Reform—An Establishment of KWAP

Many countries have embarked on pension reform. An institutional capacity to administer and implement a new system to replace the current one is one of the cornerstones in reforming any pension scheme (Darmaraj, 2017). Since KWAP is an organisation appointed by the Malaysian government to manage its retirement funds, the introduction in detail of KWAP is one of the crucial parts.

KWAP was founded in 2007 to help the Malaysian government with the transition. However, although it has grown its assets to RM141 billion as of the end of 2017 from RM42 billion in March 2007, its fund size is insufficient to reduce the government's public pension burden over the long term (Yeap, 2019).

As stated in the KWAP Annual Report 2007, KWAP is intended to assist the Federal government with payments of pension liabilities. Hence, by establishing KWAP, the Malaysian government has started a pre-funding programme to lessen its future financial obligation. The Malaysian government currently provides all of the pre-funding, which may not be sufficient to support the growing number of retirees. Additionally, administrative tasks like setting personal accounts and keeping track of contributions require some administrative readiness (Holzmann & Hinz, 2005).

In general, the duties of KWAP include establishing the pension fund's policy, overseeing the collection of contributions, supervising the execution and monitoring of investments, maintaining member accounts, and overseeing the financial administration and payment process (KWAP, 2007). Therefore, the KWAP establishment is part of Malaysia's institutional framework for a DB pension fund for public employees. Thus, a study to enhance pension sustainability for KWAP is needed in the long run.

1.4 Issues and Challenges to the Pension System

First Issue: Longevity Risk

People tend to live longer than a few decades ago (United Nations, 2019). The higher life expectancy is due to medical advancements, a better standard of living, and health awareness. Similarly, according to the latest report on life expectancy by DOSM (2021), Malaysia has improved life expectancy at birth among Malaysians since a few years ago.

According to Table 1.2, Malaysians can expect to live an average of 72.8 years for males and 78.2 years for females at birth in 2021. The average life expectancy at birth gradually grew from 72.3 years in 2000 to 74.5 years in 2010 and 75.6 years in 2021 (DOSM, 2021). The life expectancy in 2021 shows that male and female life expectancy at birth has increased by 2.8 and 3.5 years since 2000.

A study by Park and Estrada (2012) indicates that Malaysians expect to live to an average age of 80.1 between 2045 and 2050. Additionally, according to DOSM (2021), by 2030, more than 30% of Malaysians are anticipated to be older than 65, making Malaysia a fast ageing society.

Table 1.2 Life expectancy at the birth, Malaysia, 2000–2021

Year / (Years)	*2000*	*2008*	*2010*	*2019*	*2020*	*2021*
Average	72.3	74.0	74.5	74.8	75.1	75.6
Male	70.0	71.6	71.9	72.5	72.8	72.8
Female	74.7	76.4	77.0	77.4	77.8	78.2

According to the United Nations Department of Economics and Social Affairs statistics, Fig. 1.1 shows 5.02 million Malaysians aged 65 and over in 2020. That figure is expected to rise to approximately 6.96 million, 12.35 million, 15.53 million, and 16.67 million in 2030, 2050, 2070, and 2100, respectively (United Nations, 2019).

Generally, this development indicates that people are expected to have a more extended retirement. Since retirees are expected to live longer, it will increase the number of people receiving retirement benefits. This circumstance will undoubtedly increase the financial pressure on pension providers like the Malaysian government since the pension scheme secures financial security in old age. The higher life expectancy affects the cost of financing pensions and indirectly affects the pension system's sustainability.

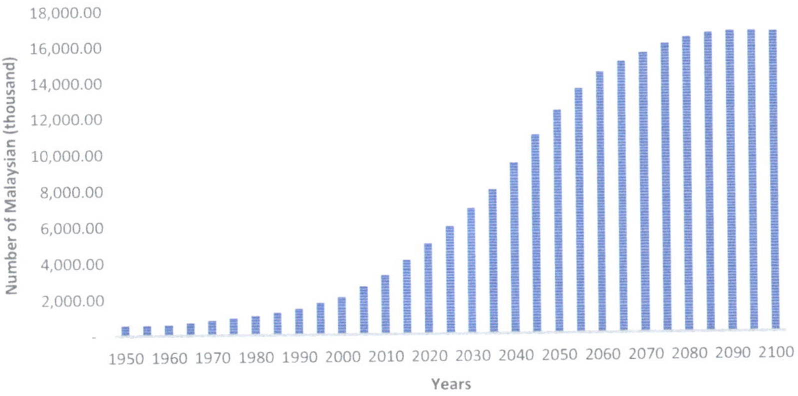

Fig. 1.1 Number of Malaysians aged 60 years old and above

As a pension provider, the Malaysian government must acknowledge the risk that people typically live longer than the number of years the pension plan anticipated. As a result, the Malaysian government has to support pensioners for a more extended retirement period due to increased post-retirement life as life expectancy increases. Palacios and Whitehouse (2006) assert that civil servants in developing countries had a longer life expectancy than the general population. According to the findings, Malaysia is exposed to longevity risk.

Besides Malaysia, pension plans in almost all countries face longevity risks (Hudson, 2007). The pension provider needs to prepare to deal with or even hedge this risk in the future. Each country has a different pension structure for dealing with this risk. Malaysia's pension structure defined the pension age as 55 years for five decades until September 2001 (Moorthy et al., 2012). The mandatory retirement age was raised to 56 in October 2001. In 2014, with a retirement age of 60 and a life expectancy of 74 years, each pensioner's payout had to last for more than 14 years. The mismatch has increased further due to a longer life expectancy, putting pressure on pension providers who risk longer and more uncertain post-retirement periods.

For Malaysia's civil servant pension scheme, payments are paid for the rest of the retiree's life. The annuity is paid to their spouse and dependent children after the retiree's death. Hence, increasing life expectancy places additional financial strains on DC pension schemes. As a result of these mounting demands, both developed and emerging nations are overhauling their pension systems. Since DB pension schemes make up the majority of public service pension plans globally, the government has been forced to review its pension plans and explore change in light of changing demographics and rising costs. However, parametric reform in the civil service pension plan may result in costs like increased wages and longer employment years, which would raise pensions even further in the future (Palacios & Whitehouse, 2006).

Second Issue: Financial Obligation to the Malaysian Government

A pension plan's ability to remain solvent depends on the annuity provider's ability to fulfil short- and long-term pension payment obligations. The ability to finance the existing debt that supports current pensions is referred to as a short-term commitment. Meanwhile, the long-term commitment is the ability to fund existing and future pension payments considering future expenditures and revenues (Barr & Diamond, 2009; Holzmann et al., 2004).

The Malaysian government faces an increasing financial burden regarding the total pensions and gratuities payable. The government owes pension obligations for the civil officials' pensions and gratuities. According to economic reports, Malaysia's expenditure on pensions and gratuities has risen yearly (MOF, 2019). According to Barr and Diamond (2009), any pension expenditure must align with the nation's capacity to pay for retirees' consumption, the investment return from the pension assets, and the fund manager's capacity to generate income in the future.

The mismatch between revenues and federal expenditure will only increase Federal debt to sustain annual operating expenditure. In 2019, the data showed that the Federal government's debt was 57.2% of the Gross Domestic Product (GDP) (MOF, 2020).. The amount of debt puts financial stabiFlity and the ability to make payments in danger. This situation may concern foreign investors (Reinhart & Rogoff, 2010).

Figure 1.2 shows that the trend has been rising. The pension cost was only about RM 6.81 billion in 2005 compared to RM 27.50 billion in 2022. The fiscal situation continues to be a concern at the macroeconomic level. Malaysia's performance in balancing expenditures and revenues has been dismal. While operating expenditures pay for present consumption, development expenditures help the nation's productive capability. Significant pension spending is unsustainable due to crucial revenue growth and economic expansion (Barr & Diamond, 2009). It may trigger a crisis and induce the government to impose more taxes or reduce expenditures elsewhere (Holzmann & Hinz, 2005). Malaysia implemented the goods and services tax (GST) in 2015 to increase revenue. However, there has not been much done to address additional leakages or reform the way emoluments and pensions are paid for.

The continuous budget deficit stems mainly from operating expenditures for Malaysia's budget. Salaries and benefits comprise the largest portion of operating expenses, typically accounting for a quarter or more of total operating costs. Emoluments made up almost 27.5% of operating expenses in 2011. The percentages have increased from 29.2% in 2012 to 28.9% in 2013 and 29.6% in 2019 (MOF, 2019).

Malaysia's operating expenditure has been increasing gradually, mainly to finance government operational expenses, including emoluments, pensions, and supplies and services. Figure 1.3 shows Malaysia's operating expenditure was almost RM107.69 billion in 2006. Since then, it

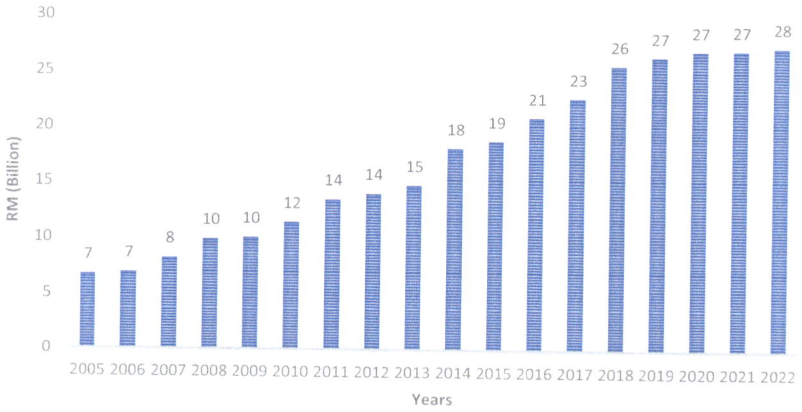

Fig. 1.2 Malaysia pension expenditure 2005–2022

has increased to nearly RM218 billion (2017), RM236 billion (2018), and RM260 billion (2019). RM297 billion, or 18.4% of the GDP, was allotted for Budget 2020; of that amount, RM241 billion, or 81.1%, was used for operating expenditures. The remaining RM56 billion was used for the development budget (MOF, 2019).

Fig. 1.3 Malaysia operating expenditure 2005–2022

The salary and emoluments play a big impact on pensions. The years of service and the last drawn salary determined the monthly pension amount. The amount allocated for emoluments as a percentage of operating expenditure has been significant over the years. For the past 15 years, emoluments accounted for more than 25% of the total operating expenditure at 26.18% in 2005, 30.77% in 2010, and 35.39% in 2017 (MOF, 2019).

The Malaysian government must be concerned about this issue to ensure long-term pension sustainability. The situation is due to the substantial increase of more than 200% in the emolument cost borne by the Federal government from RM25.59 billion in 2005 to RM82.60 billion in 2020. Given that the government pension scheme is funded using its general revenue, it thus represents a substantial operating cost to the government.

However, effective in 2013, the government implemented an automatic annual pension increment of 2% without reviewing the remuneration system or salary adjustments. It is fiscally unsustainable for the government to continue with this practice due to other committed expenses, such as debt service charges that form a substantial operating expenditure. At the same time, many people might not be adequately prepared for the high living expenses due to inflation and rising costs yearly. They would find it challenging to pay for necessities.

In Budget 2020, tabled to the Malaysia Parliament in October 2019, civil servant pension would cost the Federal government around RM27.1 billion, increasing from RM26.6 billion in 2019 (MOF, 2020). While the annual budget for 2022 saw an increase to RM28 billion (MOF, 2021). This budget includes the annual increment and pension payments to new pensioners and beneficiaries. In addition to bearing the financial burden, the Malaysian government has assisted pensioners in managing the rising cost of living, including raising the minimum monthly pension and providing them with special cash support once a year since 2010 (MOF, 2020). Due to the substantial pressure it places on the government's financial condition, the civil servant pension plan would eventually become unaffordable if this trend persists.

An increasing pension deficit over time would signify that the fund is insufficient to cover future obligations and may not be sustainable. Pension deficits and financing gaps are expressed as a percentage of GDP. When the pension fund cannot pay its short-term obligations, the gap illustrates the pension debt as a percentage of the GDP the government will have to support (Yi, 2011).

The numerous goals of a pension system, such as consumption smoothing and insurance for uncertainties and hazards, must be considered, notwithstanding requests for reform (Barr & Diamond, 2006). The World Bank has observed that other fundamental objectives are equally vital in the framework for change. These objectives include sufficiency, affordability, and resilience (Holzmann & Hinz, 2005).

Ultimately, the Federal Constitution safeguards the pension system, and the government guarantees solvency. That is assets must equal or exceed liabilities (Lee, 1997). The pension system, however, becomes unsustainable when the pension deficit is too large and continues, necessitating a review and modification of the pension parameters to assure sustainability. Recent studies have looked at the long-term sustainability of the civil service pension fund managed by the KWAP (Abdul Rahman & Lau, 2023; Irfan & Lau, 2024)

Third Issue: Number of Government Servants

The bloated size of Malaysia's civil service, which has a considerably larger ratio of city officials to the population and so results in a higher emolument expenditure, has frequently been brought up. The size of the civil service was kept at 1.7 million as of March 2019 (Abas, 2019), and 94% of positions were filled (Daim & Yunus, 2021). These civil servants are offered to have lifetime pension benefits.

In contrast, 50% of the Malaysian labour force are EPF recipients. Holzmann (2014) discusses that even Civil Servant pension plans cover only up to 10% of the labour force. However, they account for a significant amount of the income used to pay pensions. The purpose behind pensions is to attract new talents loyal to the government, particularly in the DB pension scheme, where the benefits are based on the service member's last salary (Barr & Diamond, 2006).

The differences in pension benefits favour employees in the public sector versus the private sector. Public servants receive lifelong benefits after retirement despite not contributing to their pension fund. On the other hand, under the EPF system, members contribute to their retirement fund to earn annual dividends (Narayanan, 2002). Thus, the pension scheme is the main attraction for people to join the public service.

Additionally, various allowances received by public sector employees are exempt from income tax, in contrast to those received by private sector employees, who must pay taxes on them. Since this arrangement provides a clear advantage to the labour force in the public sector, "any further advantages through pension" are "unjustified compensation differential and unnecessarily increase the cost to the government" (Palacios & Whitehouse, 2006).

The gap in labour demand between the public service and private sector also interferes with the efficient operation of the Malaysian labour market by limiting the inter-sector mobility of workers (Onozawa, 1991). The public pension vesting period restricts the mobility of civil servants, thus limiting the financial flexibility needed for labour adjustments amid economic shocks or structural changes. The eligibility period is the expense to the government for keeping employees on staff until the eligibility term is completed.

Thus, the growth in salary and pension payments outpaced productivity growth. As government-linked enterprises (GLCs) entered the private sector, the employment trend in the public sector increased (Singaravellloo, 2012). The Malaysia Ninth Plan (2006–2010) saw the growth in public sector employment recover to a 3.3% annual average growth rate (Abd Awang et al., 2010). This trend continued under the Malaysia Eleventh Plan (2016–2020) (Nixon et al., 2017).

By addressing the overlap of tasks between departments and agencies, the suggested plan aims to, among other things, reduce the size of the government service and compensation rises in industries with increased productivity. Also, rationalising open positions, maximising human resources, outsourcing, looking for alternative service delivery channels, privatisation, technology integration, and hiring based on needs, this reduction would be accomplished (Daim & Yunus, 2021).

Fourth Issue: Household Debt Among Pensioners

Mercer (2021) has recommended in the report "Pension reform in challenging times" that Malaysia improve its retirement scheme by raising household savings and lowering household debt. Due to this suggestion, the Malaysian retirement scheme's adequacy and sustainability scores and the overall index value will increase.

Out of 43 different retirement systems, Malaysia's retirement system was ranked third in Asia and 23rd globally in 2020 (Mercer, 2021). The study uses three weighted sub-indices to evaluate the sufficiency, sustainability, and integrity of each of the 43 distinct retirement plans. However, Malaysia's overall index value decreased from 60.1 in 2020 to 59.6 in 2021 despite having a better and higher ranking.

However, Mercer (2019) reported differently in the previous year. The 2019 Melbourne Mercer Global Pension Index report stated that Malaysia's pension assets increased, and individuals feel wealthier, encouraging them to borrow more. This situation makes people have a higher debt compared to the previous year. Pension assets are highly correlated with net household debt. The 2019 pension index confirmed and provided evidence for the wealth impact, a propensity for spending to increase with wealth.

The improvement in Malaysia's index rating in 2019 and 2020 shows that the system has some useful features. However, adjustments can improve long-term sustainability and benefit the people. The updated data on the Organisation for Economic Co-operation and Development (OECD) net replacement caused Malaysia's rating to improve, as governments need to ensure the pension schemes include everyone so that the whole workforce has savings for the future. However, the household debt level will only be the inverse of the household savings for retirement. Moreover, both years explored the importance of pension sustainability in the reports.

1.5 Sustainability of the Pension System

The World Bank (2008) evaluates a variety of overall pension system architectures in its policy framework. Furthermore, one of the primary criteria is affordability, which refers to whether people and society can fund the pension system without disproportionately competing with other social or economic needs or having unsustainable financial effects.

Hence, the idea behind this study is to explore the sustainability Malaysian government can keeping up with the pension plans that benefit current and future retirees. In another way, are the pension plans running out of cash or reserve in the near term? The concern is how long the plan can continue to serve and pay the benefits if there are no other investment returns, additional contributions, or any expansion of the benefit structure. At the current level, the Malaysian government shall continue to contribute, notwithstanding the basic ratio, to reflect the changes over time. As the baby boomers retire, there is an expectation that the plan will generate returns on assets and the benefit payout will increase. As a result, the book will address the following questions:

a. What are the determinants of pension cost?
b. What are the asset allocation and performance of pension schemes?
c. Can the future assets of the pension meet its future liabilities?
d. What is the long-term sustainability of the civil service pension scheme?
e. Does longevity bonds answer Malaysia's pension woe?

1.6 Significance of the Study

Despite growing concerns about the financial viability of the Civil Servant DB plan, there is a shortage of literature examining the structure or potential consequences. Globally, there have undergone unprecedented changes in longevity trends. The urge to accept the risk of post-retirement years that are longer and more uncertain has increased as longevity has grown and become more defined.

The government, non-governmental organisations (NGOs), researchers, and policymakers may utilise this study's findings as guides when examining and revising the current pension policy. This study also considers the Malaysian population's increasing cost of living and life expectancy. This research will help the Malaysian government decide the specific matter regarding pension annuities for a better standard of living for retirees. Hence, the significant study may cover a few areas:

Pension Study in Malaysia

This research could initiate new studies on pensions based on recent findings while improving the Malaysian pension scheme. The results of this study will offer a new government pension plan that, despite the existence of longevity risk, may provide future financial benefits for government civil servants or retirees that are more favourable. This new government pension must help reduce the government's financial burden while maintaining or increasing the size of the civil service workforce.

KWAP's Financial Status

One of the purposes of this study is to investigate the viability of lowering and reducing the government's pension liabilities. The findings will benefit the Ministry of Finance (MOF), KWAP, and Pension Department under Malaysia's Public Services Department. The government could refer to the result of this study for guidance in establishing a better welfare state for Malaysians. Based on the literature, several types of research have been done on KWAP, but no study has investigated KWAP's sustainability.

Longevity Bond in Malaysia's Capital Market

The impact of raising the retirement age on pension liability from 1991 to 2000 was briefly mentioned in earlier studies on civil service pension plans and the rising costs of sustaining such plans (Ibrahim et al., 2012; Lee, 1997). However, no research has examined the civil service pension plan or attempted to determine the system's viability given anticipated demographic and economic changes.

Although the size of the pension deficit is likely to increase in the future based on the trend, this area has not attracted much research. As a result, this study aims to close gaps in the existing research. This study's evaluation of the current pension system may help people better comprehend the civil service pension plan by providing more significant insights into its current structure, flaws, and potential remedial actions. The analysis in this study will also pinpoint the measures that can increase and improve the pension scheme's fiscal viability.

1.7 Chapter Organisation

This book explores various issues on the defined benefit pension fund that the Malaysian government currently confronts. Chapter 1 provides an overview of the pension system in Malaysia, covering only the civil service pension fund managed by the Retirement Fund (Incorporated), better known as KWAP. It introduces the five-pillar model of pensions and Malaysia's pension scheme. It also discusses the issues and challenges the pension system and pensioners face.

Chapter 2 discusses the issue and factors determining Malaysia's pension cost. This chapter starts by modelling the determinants of pension costs in Malaysia through data gathered from 1971 to 2020. This study discusses the sustainability factors of investment returns and pension obligations through pension-funded ratio, pension asset allocation investment, and pension-required return.

Chapter 3 examines the asset allocation and performance of the KWAP pension fund from the last 13 years since the Ministry of Finance established it as part of the pension reform.

As investment income is one of the primary sources to sustain a pension scheme by KWAP, the pension fund's asset allocation is examined and how it impacts fund return.

Based on the available pension assets and liabilities data, Chapter 4 outlines the steps and makes the 10-year forecast to ascertain whether the pension fund will be underfunded or not in the future. This chapter reviews the long-term pension-funded status for KWAP in maintaining liabilities for the next ten years. Based on the pension-funded ratio, it concludes that the civil servant pension scheme will be underfunded for the next ten years.

Chapter 5 examines whether the pension fund is sustainable in the long run based on the four parameters using scenario-based simulation. This chapter explores the required return for the Retirement Fund to maintain the pension scheme. Scenario analysis has been implied based on four inputs of contribution rate, retirement age, life expectancy, and years of service in civil servants in calculating the required return. In order to solve this problem, especially the longevity risk, Chapter 6 proposes issuing longevity bonds by the authority to mitigate the longevity risk faced by the KWAP pension fund. The applicability of longevity bonds in the Malaysian Capital Market is examined in this chapter.

Finally, the findings from Chapters 2 to 6 are summarised in Chapter 7. The conclusion and recommendations for further research were discussed in this chapter. These findings are discussed in the context of implications for improving the Malaysia Civil Servant Pension Scheme. This book is an interesting compilation of facts, analysis, and insights from this hotly debated issue the current government faces. It can be a reference for the financial market industry, regulators, market practitioners, analysts, researchers, government authorities, and universities.

References

Abas, A. (2019, April 30). Government to reduce number of public service Jobs by 5%. *New Strait Times (NST)*. https://www.nst.com.my/news/government-public-policy/2019/04/484308/171-million-civil-servants-govt-payroll-march-2019

Abd Awang, H., Ismail, R., & Mohd Noor, Z. (2010). Training impact on employee's job performance: A self evaluation. *Economic Research-Ekonomska Istraživanja, 23*(4), 78–90.

Abdul Rahman, M. I., & Lau, W.Y. (2023). Is the KWAP defined benefit pension fund sustainable in the long run? *International Journal of Banking and Finance, 18*(2), 97–126. https://doi.org/10.32890/ijbf2023.18.2.5

Barr, N., & Diamond, P. (2006). The economics of pensions. *Oxford Review of Economic Policy, 22*(1), 15–39. https://doi.org/10.1093/oxrep/grj002

Barr, N., & Diamond, P. (2009). Reforming pensions: Principles, analytical errors and policy directions. *International Social Security Review, 62*(2), 5–29. https://doi.org/10.1111/j.1468-246X.2009.01327.x

Daim, N., & Yunus, A. (2021, September 28). Pension payments to reach RM46.6bil in 2030. *New Strait Times (NST)*. https://www.nst.com.my/news/nation/2021/09/731632/pm-pension-payments-reach-rm466bil-2030

Darmaraj, S. R. (2017). *The long-term financial sustainability of the civil service pension scheme in Malaysia*. Universiti Sains Malaysia.

DOSM. (2021). Department of statistics Malaysia press release abridged life tables, Malaysia, 2019–2021. *DOSM*, *July*, 4. https://www.dosm.gov.my/v1/index.php?r=column/pdfPrev&id=R0VPdE1mNEdRQms2S0M4M1ZsSlVEdz09

Holzmann, R. (2014). Old-age financial protection in Malaysia: Challenges and options old-age. *Social Protection & Labor Discussion Paper Series*, *1425*, 1–30. www.worldbank.org/spl.

Holzmann, R., & Hinz, R. (2005). Old-Age income support in the 21st Century. In *Old-Age Income Support in the 21st Century* (Issue January 2005). https://doi.org/10.1596/0-8213-6040-x

Holzmann, R., Palacios, R., & Zviniene, A. (2004). *Implicit pension debt: issues, measurement and scope in international perspective*. *0403*, 38. http://documents.worldbank.org/curated/en/947731468762352221/Implicit-pension-debt-issues-measurement-and-scope-in-international-perspective

Hudson, R. (2007). Longevity risk: A new global market? *Journal of Risk Management in Financial Institutions, 1*(1), 74–89.

Ibrahim, R. I. (2012). Impact of increasing retirement age on longevity factor: An empirical study for government pensioners in Malaysia. *Jurnal Ekonomi Malaysia*, *46*(2), 29–35.

Irfan, M., & Lau, W.-Y. (2024). Asset allocation and performance of Malaysian civil service pension fund, *Australasian Accounting, Business and Finance Journal, 18*(1), 86–107. https://doi.org/10.14453/aabfj.v18i1.06
JPA. (2021). *Malaysia Pension Scheme*. Bahagian Pasca Perkhidmatan. http://www.jpapencen.gov.my/english/pension_scheme.html
KWAP. (2007). KWAP Annual Report 2007. *KWAP Website*. https://www.kwap.gov.my/EN/UsefulInformation/Publication/AnnualReports/KWAPAnnualReport2007.pdf
KWAP. (2011). KWAP Annual Report 2011. *Kumpulan Wang Persaraan (diperbadankan), 82*(10), 4.
KWAP. (2017). KWAP Annual Report 2017. *KWAP Website*. https://www.kwap.gov.my/EN/UsefulInformation/Publication/AnnualReports/KWAPAnnualReport2017.pdf
KWAP. (2018). KWAP Annual Report 2018. *KWAP Website, 86*(3), 64–65. https://www.kwap.gov.my/EN/UsefulInformation/Publication/AnnualReports/KWAPAnnualReport2017.pdf
KWAP. (2019). *Background KWAP*. https://www.kwap.gov.my/en/
Malaysian Law. (2007). Act 662 Retirement Fund Act 2007. *Malaysia, December*.
Lee, K. C. (1997). The Malaysian Government Pension Scheme. Whither Its Future Direction ? *Jurnal Ekonomi Malaysia, 31*, 87–106.
LTAT. (2022). *Corporate Profile LTAT*. LTAT. https://www.ltat.org.my/ltat/corporate-profile/
Lucas, J. R. E., Lucas, R. E., & Gillman, M. (1990). Supply-Side economics: An analytical review. *Collected Papers on Monetary Theory*, 331–360.
Mercer. (2019). *Global Pension.*
Mercer. (2021). Pension Reform in Challenging Times. In *Mercer CFA Institute Global Pension Index, 69*(5).
Ministry of Finance, Malaysia (MOF). (2021). *Malaysia Budget 2022.*
Ministry of Finance, Malaysia (MOF). (2020). *Estimated Federal Expenditure 2021.* http://belanjawan2021.treasury.gov.my/index.php/en/ap-2021
Ministry of Finance, Malaysia (MOF). (2019). Malaysia 2020 budget speech by YB Tuan Lim Guan Eng. *Parliament Malaysia, October 2019*, 1–13.
Moorthy, M. K., Durai, T., Chelliah, L., Sien, C. S., Leong, L. C., Kai, N. Z., Rhu, W. C., & Teng, W. Y. (2012). A Study on the Retirement Planning Behaviour of Working Individuals in Malaysia. *International Journal of Academic Research in Economics and Management Sciences, 1*(2), 54.
Narayanan, S. (2002). Old age support for private sector employees in Malaysia.pdf. *Hitotsubashi Journal of Economics, 43*, 119–134.
Nixon, S., Asada, H., & Koen, V. (2017). *Fostering Inclusive Growth in Malaysia.*
OECD. (2020). Pension Funds in Figures 2020. *Oecd, June*, 1–5.
Onozawa, J. (1991). Restructuring of employment patterns under the new economic policy. *The Developing Economies, 29*(4), 314–329.

Palacios, R., & Whitehouse, E. (2006). Civil-Service pension schemes around the world. In *Social Protection Discussion Paper* (Issue 14796). http://mpra.ub.uni-muenchen.de/14796/1/primer_0602.pdf

Park, D., & Estrada, G. E. B. B. (2012). Developing Asia's pension systems and old-age income support. In *SSRN Electronic Journal* (Issue 358). https://doi.org/10.2139/ssrn.2052668

Reinhart, C. M., & Rogoff, K. S. (2010). Growth in a time of debt. *American Economic Review, 100*(2), 573–578. https://doi.org/10.1257/aer.100.2.573

Retirement Fund Act (2007) (Act 662). http://www.iicm.org.my/wp-content/uploads/2019/04/KWAp-Compliance-with-II-Code-31-Dec-2018.pdf

Singaravellloo, K. (2012). Redefining relationships: Privatisation and public-private partnerships. In *Public Management and Governance in Malaysia* (p. 20).

The World Bank. (2008). The World Bank pension conceptual framework. *World Bank Pension Reform Primer, 202*, 8. http://hdl.handle.net/10986/11139

United Nations, D. of E. A. S. D. and P. (2019). *World Mortality 2019*. 24.

Yeap, C. (2019, October 3). Public pension reform painful, necessary, overdue. *The Edge Markets*. https://www.theedgemarkets.com/article/cover-story-public-pension-reform-painful-necessary-overdue

Yi, Z. (2011). Effects of demographic and retirement-age policies on future pension deficits, with an application to China. *Population and Development Review, 37*(3), 553–569. https://doi.org/10.1111/j.1728-4457.2011.00434.x

CHAPTER 2

Determinants of Pension Cost

2.1 Introduction

Income security during the post-retirement period is one of the biggest social and economic concerns in the twenty-first century. The issue has brought much attention to discussing pension sustainability around the world. The Malaysian government has started raising concerns about the rising pension cost trend over the past few years. Due to that circumstance, the Malaysian government is considering replacing permanent and pension schemes for public service appointments with contractual appointments.

The Malaysian government clarified that the contractual appointment would offer public servants better pay, welfare, and protection. The new scheme is protected under the Public Service Act. It covers civil servants' permanent or contractual interests to ensure they would not be quickly terminated without being proven guilty in severe circumstances.

This new idea is to reduce the future burden of sustaining pension liabilities. However, Malaysia is still looking for the best solution to tackle public concerns regarding pension payments. The government is trying to balance out the ability to continue to pay so public servants do not lose out in the surviving post-retirement period.

A pension scheme aims to provide future economic security to retirees and their survivors after retiring in the event of death or due to permanent disability. As the fertility rate drops and the ageing society develops over

M. I. Abdul Rahman and W. Y. Lau, *Pension at Stake*,
https://doi.org/10.1007/978-981-97-2324-9_2

the years, Holzmann and Hinz (2005) have developed the World Bank's Pension Conceptual Framework under the auspices of the World Bank and the World Bank's five-pillar system. The World Bank (2008) designed the five-pillar model, defining the range of design elements to provide a scheme of the five-pillar model to classify the various ways to fund the retirement system.

Regardless of the pillars, country-specific constraints necessitate executing a basic and carefully sequenced approach that will narrow the viable possibilities significantly. Each country needs to determine the pension system modalities and reform options. In Malaysia, the pension structure is composed of three main retirement schemes.

The first is the Civil Service Pension Scheme managed by the Kumpulan Wang Persaraan (Diperbadankan) or Retirement Fund (Incorporated), better known as KWAP by the public. In short, KWAP is a statutory body which manages the pension scheme for Malaysia's public employees. The second being the Kumpulan Wang Simpanan Pekerja (KWSP) or Employee Provident Fund (EPF). The last one is the Lembaga Tabung Angkatan Tentera (LTAT) or Armed Forces Fund Board.

Malaysia Defined Benefit Pension Scheme

The number of Malaysian public sector employees keeps rising yearly, although a dwindling increment rate has been observed. As of the third quarter of 2019, Malaysian public servants currently stand at about 1.7 million employees if the armed forces and police force are included (Abas, 2019). The number consists of the federal and state-level service staff, national and state-level statutory bodies, and local authorities—where 62% are employed in the health, education, military, and police sectors.

The public sector has been rising as government jobs offer an attractive package. In terms of perks, the civil servant pension scheme is one of the unique features provided by the Malaysian government. Besides the stable tenure, other factors such as housing government loans, medical benefits extending to families, opportunities for further studies, and various allowances offered are often perceived as attractive. The Malaysian civil service is known to have a one-fits-all system for compensation and benefits that applies throughout the public sector (Abd Manaf, 2011).

Abd Manaf (2011) deliberated that the service pension scheme is a legacy of the British administration introduced in 1875. The pension scheme is a non-contributory scheme that supports public servants after they retire and their dependents (spouses and minor children) upon their death. The aim is to compensate for the permanent loss of financial support for dependents among public servants. Currently, the scheme is run by the Malaysia Pensions Department and is funded by government employees. At the same time, Retirement Fund (Incorporated) (KWAP) acts as an agent appointed by the Ministry of Finance (MOF) for fund collection and management (Retirement Fund Act, 2007).

Formal economic research on the incentives built into pension systems began around 1970 (Clark et al., 2003). Employers utilise pension plans to attract, keep, motivate, and retire people, as well as the plan, which is a significant aspect of remuneration from the firm perspective. Individually, financial security in old age necessitates two instruments: a consumption smoothing mechanism and a means of insurance (Barr & Diamond, 2006).

Defined benefit and defined contribution plans are the two most common pension plans. Defined benefit plans promise workers a specified benefit at retirement based on years of service, annual earnings, and position in an organisation. In defined contribution plans, the employer and the worker make a periodic contribution, and the investment returns accrued during work. Most public and private pension schemes have historically offered defined benefit plans. However, in the last quarter of the twentieth century, there was a significant trend from defined benefit plans to defined contribution plans (Clark & McDermed, 1990; Clark et al., 2003; Gustman & Steinmeier, 1992).

After a few revisions, Malaysia's latest retirement age is 60. The civil servant pension's structure defined the pension age as revised from 55 to 58 years in 2001 after five decades. However, the pension age was revised from 58 to 60 in 2012.

Besides the government pension scheme, two prominent pension schemes in Malaysia are the Employee Provident Fund (EPF) and the Armed Personnel Fund Board (LTAT). The EPF manages a defined contributions pension scheme for private employees, and the LTAT oversees specific industries' compulsory and voluntary pension contributions for non-pensionable and pensionable armed forces. This study does not discuss the EPF and LTAT pension schemes. The Private Retirement Scheme and the Basic State Scheme are also not discussed.

Financial Burden

Since the Malaysian government pension provides an essential source of income to a civil servant in any contingency, the pension scheme is financially viable. It must adequately finance to continue paying the expected benefits as stipulated in the pension laws in the future. Due to that, the Malaysian government faces an increasing financial burden regarding the total annual amount of pensions and gratuities payable. The pensions and gratuities payable to its employees are pension liabilities to the government.

According to economic reports, expenditure on pensions and gratuities has risen. The latest 2021 budget estimates that federal pension expenditure will cost about $ 27 billion (MOF, 2020). Figure 2.1 shows that the pension cost has been rising exponentially.

In 2013, the government implemented an annual pension increment of 2% without waiting for any review of the remuneration system or salary adjustments. It is fiscally unsustainable for the government to continue on this path, given that other committed expenses, such as debt service charges, take the lion's share of operating expenditure.

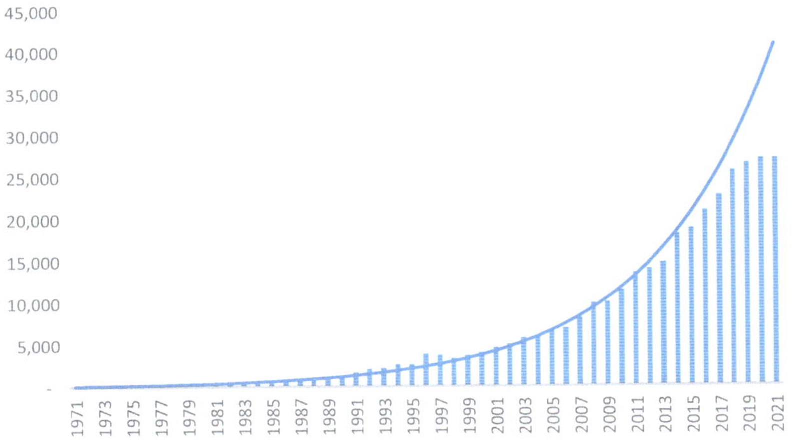

Fig. 2.1 Trend of Malaysia's annual pension cost 1971–2021 (*Source* Various Economic Reports)

Under the defined benefit pension system, the civil servant does not need to contribute or save towards their pension; hence, longevity is not an issue because public pension payments are tax-funded in Malaysia. However, longevity is a risk for the government. To help in this trap, the Malaysian government has taken a step forward by revising the retirement age from 55 to 56, starting in October 2001. Further down the road, Malaysia's compulsory retirement age has been changed for the second time from 56 to 58 years old with an additional clause to allow an option to retire earlier, starting July 2008.

A higher estimation for retirement cost at RM26.6 billion (2019) will be increased to RM27.1 billion (2020) due to annual increments to accommodate the rising number of pensioners and beneficiaries. For the past fifty years, the rates of growth of pension payments for the period Malaysia pension cost have been rising yearly. Pension costs doubled every ten years. It recorded an increase of 535% from 1971 to 1980. This trend was followed by an increase of 101% from 1981 to 1990. Lastly, there was an increase of 131% from 1991 to 2000. The millennia years from 2000 to 2010 have slightly increased from 144%, and the last decade from 2010 to 2020 recorded a 99.8% increase to RM27 billion. The growth rate of pension payments from 1971 to 2020 fluctuated between negative 9.3 (1997 to 1998) and 83.3% (1977 to 1978).

The Malaysian government has acknowledged that pension payments have become a substantial financial burden even though they agreed to maintain the civil servants' pension scheme. Hence, any future pension bill that involves salary increments among civil servants should consider the government's financial strength. However, a new mechanism has yet to be explored to alleviate the burden on the nation's coffers. A fundamental question is whether the Malaysian government is running out of resources to maintain the current pension scheme for public servants. Whether our current pension system still needs to be improvised or not. Alternatively, the Malaysian government needs to review current system features to sustain the pension scheme in the long run.

This remaining part of the study is organised as follows. Section 2.2 reviews the literature, followed by the data and methodology. Section 4 discusses the result, and the last section concludes our study.

Malaysia Pension Studies

Historically, the Malaysian civil service formed the most significant employer during the early post-colonisation era, employing about 300,000 or 16% of total employment (Abd Manaf, 2011). The number increased more than double when it reached almost 700,000 people in 1997. However, the public sector growth rate has reduced to between 0.35 and 0.64% by the 1990s. Public sector privatisation introduced by the Malaysian government in 1983 and then intensified in later years has significantly slowed down the public sector job growth (Lee, 1997).

In terms of perks, the civil servant pension scheme is one of the Malaysian government's unique features. Abd Manaf (2011) deliberated that the service pension scheme is a legacy of the British administration, introduced in 1875. The Malaysian public pension also acknowledges the importance of providing survivor benefits, which are of immediate concern to the welfare of employees' families.

However, Ibrahim (2012) believed that the current pension scheme in Malaysia needs to be reformed as it is not financially viable to sustain in the long term due to the gradual increase in the average Malaysian life expectancy. The public pension scheme must be economically feasible since it covers an essential source of income for the public servant. Otherwise, the scheme cannot continue paying the expected benefits stipulated under the Pension Act.

The result shows a growth rate of 0.9 and 1% in the early 1980s compared to that of 5.4 and 5.6% in the early 1970s. The growth rates of the size of the public sector reduced to between 0.35 and 0.64%. The trend has shown how Mahathir's idea of privatising some entities has limited the future expansion of the number of pensioners. Regarding financial viability, the pension scheme cannot merely depend solely on the tax-payer, where the government must sustain another programme in the long term.

There are two significant pension benefit plans—defined benefit (DB) and defined contribution (DC). The DB plan is the pension benefit type in which the Malaysian government guarantees pension benefits to the employee upon retirement based on the employee's final salary scale.

In the DB plan, governments as annuity providers must pay a specified annuity to retirees. The benefits are guaranteed regardless of whether the retiree's DB plan is underfunded. The benefit amounts are an obligation of the employer, irrespective of its financial condition or capacity.

Funding Pension

Funding pension plans means putting aside financial assets dedicated to making promised payments in the future. The amount of money that pension and annuity providers should set away each year is determined by how actuaries allocate expenses each year. Hence, establishing and maintaining a high level of assets relative to liabilities requires fiscal discipline and many years of planning.

Martell et al. (2013) show a meaningful reciprocal relationship between public pensions and states' finances. Thus, any government's financial health is inextricably linked to the funded status of all its DB-sponsored plans and other post-employment benefit programmes.

Three characteristics of the plan would be related to the funded ratio: when the programme started, plan size, and the generosity of benefits. When the plan begins, older plans will likely have promised benefits over a more extended period without putting aside funds to cover the promises, thereby creating a significant unfunded liability. Therefore, the older the plan, the lower the expected funded ratio.

The question of funding has been discussed urgently for two motives. First, state and local plans are holding stock markets as equities that expose market risk that might undermine the status of virtually all pension plans. Second, baby boomers are about to begin retiring in large numbers, which means that benefits are slated to increase sharply (Munnell et al., 2011).

One of the key concerns is how long state and local plans will keep their promises. In other words, are the plans going to run out of cash? Moreover, if so, when will it happen? The plan assets to benefits ratio is the most obvious place to start, which illustrates how many years the plan could continue to pay benefits if there are no other investment returns, no additional contributions, and no growth in benefits. Plan sponsors will continue to contribute, notwithstanding the basic ratio, to reflect the changes over time. As the baby boomers retire, it is hoped that plans will generate returns on their assets and that benefit payout will increase.

Abdul Rahman and Lau (2023) examine the long-term sustainability of the civil service pension fund managed by KWAP. They simulated 560 scenarios to examine the required rate of return needed to fund this defined benefit pension based on four parameters, namely contribution rate, years of service, retirement age and life expectancy. They found that the minimum years of service for pension eligibility should be increased to 20 years. In addition, a contribution rate of at least 13 percent per worker to KWAP is needed. They concluded that the contribution period is more crucial than the post-retirement period for the sustainability of the pension fund.

Factors on Pension Cost

Salary, Emolument, and Inflation Adjustment

Chee (1997) has found a few factors that contribute to this problem in terms of increasing the cost of pension financing. These factors cover the pension benefit, the salary component in pension formulae, the implementation of annual pension adjustments, increasing the number of public servants, higher life expectancy, and higher demand from existing pensioners and retirement provisions.

Since the monthly pension is calculated based on the length of public service and the last drawn salary before retirement, the compensation has highly correlated pension costs yearly. It matters as higher emoluments always reflect higher salaries for civil servants. For the past five decades, emolument has contributed over 30% of total annual operating expenditure. Based on the economic report, the emolument percentage has been increasing as recorded at 32.28% (2015), 34.78% (2016), 35.59% (2017), 34.63% (2018), 31.57% (2019), and 34.28% (2020).

The percentage contribution of emoluments to OE has been significantly enormous over the years. Emolument costs to the Malaysian government have increased by more than 200% within 15 years—from RM26 billion in 2005 to RM83 billion in 2020. Each salary revision causes a sharp increase in pensions and gratuities. For example, an additional RM93 million and RM29 million were budgeted to finance pension arrears due to salary revisions in 1980 and 1990. Furthermore, in 1990, the first allocation of RM500 million was made to the pension fund (Lee, 1997).

Even with the rising trend of pension costs, the Malaysian government has taken an incentive to help pensioners cope with rising living costs, including increasing the minimum monthly pension and giving special cash assistance since 2010 (MOF, 2019). A pension adjustment introduced under the Pension Adjustment Act 1980 reflects the government's efforts to protect the purchasing power of pensioners' income and ensure them an opportunity to share in the fruits of any economic growth enjoyed by those still working. The changes to the public service schemes would also apply to the current retirees, not just the new ones. The Malaysian government should look at this issue severely for the long-term condition.

As stated by Chee (1997), one problem of the pension government attributed to the pension formulae's benefit structure and salary component. Besides the monthly pension payment, there is no maximum limit on the gratuity paid to the pensioner. At the same time, inflation has pushed the pension payment to increase yearly, leading to demands for a higher salary while serving the nation. An increase in life expectancy can be solved by adjusting the accrued pension using the latest mortality rate while raising the later retirement age (Lindell, 2003). To maintain the current living standards, people who are now healthier may prefer to work longer than the previous generation and receive a higher monthly receive payment.

Population and Life Expectancy

In terms of population, the Malaysian population has been gradually increasing since 1950. DOSM (2018) stated that Malaysia's population increased by 2.41% annually between 1950 and 2020 United Nations (2019) predicts Malaysia's population will reach 32.4 million in 2020 compared to 31.95 million in 2018.

During the last two decades, the United Nations (2019) has shown that Malaysia's population growth is about a 36.51% increase compared to the Southeast Asian population which is approximately 25.57%. Besides the population growth, the age composition of the Malaysian population is also undergoing a noticeable transition.

The dynamic changes in the population breakdown of Malaysia over the last three decades are noticeable (DOSM, 2018). In 1990, the Malaysian population was typically distinguished by large shares of the 0- to 19-year-old youth population, with around 47.20% of the Malaysian population together. While the absolute number of the working-age population rose in 2000, these four age groups (0–19 years old) dropped to 43.17%, 38% in 2010, and 31.70% in 2020.

Hussein (2019) believes Malaysia is still facing the first demographic transition in terms of economic perspective regarding demographics. Roy (2012) believed life expectancy to have risen significantly around the globe, as much as Asia's life expectancy rate over the past 30 years.

However, DOSM (2018) explained that Malaysia is heading towards becoming an ageing nation by 2030, with more than 30% of Malaysian falling under the elderly category, 60 years old and above. The number of older people has doubled within 30 years of Malaysia's development.

Life expectancy has continued to rise significantly over the past few decades worldwide. This demographic transition model, an increase in longevity, is translated from better healthcare and higher living standards. Even the latest statistics have shown that Malaysians older than 60 will rise to 5.5 million by 2030, contributing about 14.4% of the population compared to 2.3 million (or 8.2%) in 2010 (DOSM, 2018). Another study by Yew and Cheong (2013) suggested that recent developments showed that family support as the primary care provider in older Malaysia has weakened. The UN has shown that people above 60 in Asia now make up 10% of the population, compared to 6% in 1960 (United Nations, 2019).

Contrary to popular belief, ageing is not a problem more common in developed economies. Because of rapid fertility decline and an increase in life expectancy, many developing countries have a burgeoning ageing population growing faster than developed countries but still at low per capita income levels. In terms of gender, the study done (by Moore, 1987) shows that costs to employ females compared to males are higher due to a higher life expectancy. The result demonstrated that each dollar of increased pension liabilities reduces females' salaries by fifty-five cents.

Besides, Hussein (2019) argues that declining fertility could contribute significantly to the demographic transition. The fertility rate worldwide has declined, and an increase in life expectancy has resulted in developing countries moving towards the ageing population faster than developed countries. For example, the study by United Nations (2019) has shown that ages above 60 in Asia countries is the makeup of 10% compared to 6% in 1960.

Increasing life expectancy means higher budget commitments on retirement payments and healthcare needs, as retirees are entitled to medical benefits post-retirement. With increasing life expectancy, the government has to budget for higher retirement payments and healthcare costs for pensioners. Moreover, early retirement places an unsustainable burden on pension financing. There is no easy solution, but delaying retirement could help.

On average, the world life expectancy statistics reached 72.6 years in 2019, while the number of ordinary people who survived from birth in

1990 was 64.2 years (United Nations, 2019). In Malaysia, life expectancy is higher than the average world expectancy in 2019 at 76.2 years old, while the world level is 70.2 years. However, Singapore and Thailand's life expectancy is recorded as higher than Malaysia's at 83.6 years old and 77.1 years old, respectively (United Nations, 2019).

For individuals, getting old brings various health issues and adjusting lifestyles. For families, old members require long-term care, which increases the financial burden on those working. At the national level, an ageing population demands additional resources—economic, infrastructural, and workforce—to provide social protection at the very time when the pool of contributors—those of working age—is shrinking (Yew & Cheong, 2013).

An ageing population would result in higher government expenditure, as pension payments are expected to increase as pensioners and beneficiaries will have a longer life expectancy. Therefore, this leads to an increase in pension liabilities to the Malaysian government. The rising average number of years remaining for persons of retirement represents an additional factor to be reckoned with in examining expenditure on pension benefits. Many countries and pension benefits providers have struggled to find the best solutions to decrease increased longevity on pension costs. However, some argue that increasing the compulsory retirement age will reduce the retirement span. In other words, pension liabilities will be reduced to the government—at least in the long term.

Ibrahim (2012) mentioned that many entities are looking for an optimal solution to slow down the longevity of pension costs. Retirement age amendments were uncommon before the 1990s. Instead, the trend was typical to offer an opportunity for a public servant to retire earlier than the prescribed age. However, since the 1990s, the trend has changed. As the retirement age increases, the public pension obligation will be reduced substantially, allowing the government to save substantial costs. The study/calculation done by Ibrahim (2012) shows that a decrease in longevity factors who survive is more significant than the percentage of increase in pensioners who die at a particular retirement age. Overall, longevity factors become less significant when the retirement age increases.

Lindell (2003) believed that the compulsory retirement age should be extended to help in reducing pension financing, as people living longer leads to higher public pension financing. On similar thoughts, Machnes (2000) believed an increase in contributions of society members who were still working, reducing pensioner benefits or setting a later retirement age could balance the resources in society.

Therefore, the Malaysian government has revised the retirement age from 55 to 56, starting in October 2001. Further down the road, Malaysia's compulsory retirement age has been changed for the second time from 56 to 58 years old with an additional clause to allow an option to retire earlier, starting July 2008. The latest retirement age revision was in January 2012, when the Malaysian government increased again from 58 to 60 years old for the third time. However, Ibrahim (2012) argued that the amendment retirement age could only result in higher pension expenditure as pension calculation is based on the last pay salary. The higher expenditure is to cover the extended employment services.

Economic Growth and Crisis

Since the Malaysian government pension provides an essential source of income to a civil servant in any contingency, the pension scheme is financially viable. Indeed, it must adequately finance to continue paying the expected benefits as stipulated in the pension laws in the future. However, the Malaysian government faces an increasing financial burden regarding the total pensions and gratuities payable. The pensions and gratuities payable to its employees are pension liabilities to the government. According to economic reports, expenditure on pensions and gratuities has risen yearly. In the latest budget 2020 that was tabled in Malaysia's parliament in October 2019, the civil servant pension will cost the Federal government around RM27.1 billion (MOF, 2020).

Since pension cost is under the Operating Expenditure (OPEX), the OPEX has gradually increased, mainly to finance government operational expenses, including salaries, supplies, and services.

The OPEX has grown from RM107.69 billion (2006) to nearly RM217.7 billion (2017), RM235.45 billion (2018), and RM259.85 billion (2019). According to the latest figure, a total of RM297 billion or 18.4% of the gross domestic product (GDP) will be allocated for Budget 2020, out of which 81.1% or RM241 billion is for operating expenditure (OE), while the balance of RM56 billion is for development expenditure (DE). The latest Malaysia budget has comprised an OE of RM241 billion (11% of pension cost) and development expenditure (DE) of RM56 billion.

Davis and Hu (2004) found that a positive relationship directly links pension assets and economic growth. Using the Cobb–Douglas production function, they investigated the correlation between pension assets and economic performance. The idea is based on the philosophy that pension assets can affect economic growth indirectly via financial market development (Davis, 2005; Walker & Lefort, 2000) or by its economy-wide impact through corporate engagement (Clark & Hebb, 2003) and giving rise to less labour market distortion following pension reforms (Disney, 2003).

2.2 Methodology

This study attempts to model and investigate factors influencing pension costs over an extended period in the Malaysian economy using Ordinary Least Square (OLS) annual time series data from 1971 to 2019. A conceptual framework examines the pension expenditure for the past 50 years.

As a refinement, this study will diverge from the standard pension models by selecting a few independent variables based on the current literature survey. The number of pensioners refers to retired civil servant and their dependents. Theoretically, the Malaysian Federal government categorises pension costs under Operating Expenditure (OE). The number of pensioners will influence pension costs and will answer whether the higher pension cost will lead to higher operating expenditure. They are an increase in pensioner numbers demanding benefits and retirement provisions.

The financial viability of the pension structure also depends on economic and demographic factors. Economic growth affects revenue and, hence, the taxability of the Malaysian government. In economics, inflation would pressure the government as an employer to raise salary levels in the public sector, increasing future retirees. Demographic factors such as life expectancy and mortality rates impact the number of beneficiaries on the size of the working population. The size of the public sector is also crucial as it directly determines the size of pension expenditures—implementing the Pension Adjustment Act (1980).

Hence, the list variables for independent variables (IV) and dependent variables are shown in Table 2.1 below:

Table 2.1 List of dependent and independent variables

Variables	*Description*	*Unit of measurement*	*Frequency*	*Source*
Dependent Variables (DV)				
PEC	Malaysia Annual Pension Cost	Million	Annual	Economic Report, Ministry of Finance (MoF)
OPEX	Malaysia Operating Expenditure	Million	Annual	Economic Report, Ministry of Finance (MoF)
PECOPEX	Pension Cost to Operating Expenditure	Percentage	Annual	Economic Report, Ministry of Finance (MoF)
Independent Variables (IV)				
INFL	Malaysia Consumer Price Index Rebased 2010	Points	Annual	International Monetary Fund (IMF)
NPENS	Number of Pensioners and Beneficiaries	Person	Annual	Public Service Department (PSD)
LIFEXP	Average Malaysian Life Expectancy	Years	Annual	United Nations Department of Economic and Social Affairs (UN DESA)
EMOL	Malaysia Emolument Cost	Million	Annual	Economic Report, Ministry of Finance (MoF)
MGNP	Malaysia's Gross National Product	Million	Annual	CEIC Data
POP65	Malaysia Share Population Age 65 Years and Above	Thousand	Annual	United Nations Department of Economic and Social Affairs (UN DESA)

(continued)

Table 2.1 (continued)

Variables	*Description*	*Unit of measurement*	*Frequency*	*Source*
POPG	Malaysia Population Growth Rate	Percentage	Annual	United Nations Department of Economic and Social Affairs (UN DESA)
CRISIS	Dummy Variable	Crisis = 1, 1973–74, 1986–87, 1997–98, 2008–09; other years, crisis = 0		

As shown in Table 2.1, all the data used are obtained from various sources, including Economic Report, Number of Pensioners and Beneficiaries, United Nations DESA, Department of Statistics Malaysia (DOSM), and CEIC DataStream. All series are transformed into a natural logarithm before the estimation. This study has determined three dependent variables to be studied.

On top of the independent variables, the lag-dependent variable has been used to solve the autocorrelation issue. Those variables are pension cost, operating expenditure, and percentage of pension cost to operating expenditure.

Accordingly, the mathematical function can be expressed as below:

$$\textbf{Pension Cost} = \textbf{f(INFL, NPEN, EMOL, LIFE, MGNP, POPG, POP65)} \quad (2.1)$$

where,

PEC denotes annual pension cost; INFL denotes consumer price index; EMOL denotes emolument cost; LIFE denotes average life expectancy; MGNP denotes Malaysia's Gross National Product (GNP); POPG denotes population growth; Pop65 denotes the number of the population above 65 years old.

Since Malaysia's federal budget annually presents expenditures into two categories, operating expenditure (OE) and development expenditure (DE), the Federal government categorises Malaysia's pension cost and emolument under operating expenditure (OE). The components of OE are:

$$\mathbf{OE} = \mathbf{Sum\ of\ (Emolument,\ Supplies\ and\ Services,\ Fixed\ Charges\ and\ Grants,\ Others}$$

The operating expenditure can be decomposed into several items if the formula is expanded. They are emoluments, pensions and gratuities, debt services charges, grants and transfers to the state government, supplies and services, subsidies, scholarships, and educational aid, operating grants to primary and secondary schools, asset acquisition, refund and write-offs, grants to statutory bodies, and other expenditures. Since the pension cost is part of operating expenditure, a new model can be formulated as below:

$$\mathbf{OPEX} = \mathbf{f(INFL, NPEN, EMOL, LIFE, MGNP, POPG, POP65)} \quad (2.2)$$

Notably, this study addresses whether the independent variables precede the pension cost and operating expenditure. This study has computed the rate of pension cost over the operating expenditure as a new dependent variable. The model is as below:

$$\mathbf{PECOPEX} = \mathbf{f(INFL, NPEN, EMOL, LIFE, MGNP, POPG, POP65)} \quad (2.3)$$

Hypothesis

Based on the discussion on the model, this study intends to investigate the impact of the independent variables on the pension cost that directly impacts operating expenditure.

H1: Inflation is positively related to pension cost
H2: The crisis is positively related to the pension cost
H3: The emolument is positively related to the pension cost
H4: The life expectancy is positively related to the pension cost
H5: The Malaysian population above 65 is positively associated with the pension cost
H6: The number of pensioners is positively related to the pension cost
H7: The Malaysian population growth is positively related to the pension cost

H8: The Malaysian Malaysia Gross National Product is positively associated with pension cost

The same independent variables will be tested on three dependent variables: operating expenditures, pension cost, and pension cost to operating expenditure.

2.3 Result

Descriptive Statistics

The descriptive analysis of explanatory variables and correlation matrix table is presented in Table 2.2 below.

Table 2.2 shows that all variables show an uprising trend except population growth. All variables have 49 observations from 1971 to 2019 except the number of pensioners available after 1999.

Overall, all models have shown that inflation, life expectancy, emolument, and the number of pensioners positively relate to pension cost. At the same time, the crisis has a negative impact on pension costs for all models. However, a population above 65 has a mixed direction in Model 2 and Model 5.

Table 2.3 shows that life expectancy positively relates to pension cost—Models 1, 2, and 5. The number of pensioners is also a significant variable. However, the small sample size of 20 (Model 4) might be why the module is not substantial. Hence, Model 5 is the adequate model for the dependent variable of the pension cost. Due to multicollinearity, the population growth rate and Malaysia's GNP are excluded from the model.

Table 2.4 shows that emolument positively relates to OPEX (Model 1 and 2). The number of pensioners is also significant, but the small sample size of 20 (Model 3). Model 1 is the adequate model for the dependent variable of operating expenditure. The lag-dependent variable has been used to solve the autocorrelation issue.

Table 2.5 shows that life expectancy is positively related to pension cost to OPEX (Models 1 and 2). Emolument is negatively associated with pension cost to OPEX (Model 1, 2, and 4). GNP is negatively related to pension cost to OPEX (Model 6). *The population above 65 years and above is positively associated with* pension cost to OPEX (Model 2). The number of pensioners is also significant, but due to the small sample size

Table 2.2 Descriptive statistics

Variables	*CRISIS*	*INFL*	*LIFEXP*	*LNEMOL*	*LNMGNP*	*LNNPENS*	*LNPOP65*	*POPG*
Mean	0.16	3.49	71.38	9.33	12.11	13.21	7.17	2.24
Median	0	3	71.8	9.34	12.26	13.16	7.09	2.4
Maximum	1	17.3	76.1	11.32	14.2	13.64	8.13	3.03
Minimum	0	0.3	65	6.81	9.42	12.88	6.41	1.34
Std. Dev	0.37	2.89	3.16	1.33	1.4	0.24	0.51	0.5
Skewness	1.82	2.67	−0.36	−0.22	−0.21	0.5	0.28	−0.58
Kurtosis	4.32	12.48	2.07	2.05	1.9	2.04	1.87	2.23
Jarque–Bera	30.67	241.72	2.84	2.24	2.83	1.58	3.23	3.98
Observations	49	49	49	49	49	20	49	49

Notes Sample from 1971 to 2019
Ln devotes all series have been transformed to the natural algorithm
The value in parentheses is the p-value Ln denotes all series have been transformed into natural logarithms,

Table 2.3 Dependent variable 1: Ln_Pension Cost

Independent variable	*Model*				
	(1)	*(2)*	*(3)*	*(4)*	*(5)*
Inflation	0.0146	0.0148	0.045	0.077	0.0030
	(0.40)	(0.41)	(0.46)	(0.37)	(0.86)
Crisis	−0.077	−0.078	−0.199	−-0.28	−0.10
	(0.51)	(0.51)	(0.42)	(0.41)	(0.36)
LIFEXP	0.48**	0.48**			0.31**
	(0.00)	(0.00)			(0.00)
LNEMOL	0.15	0.17			
	(0.67)	(0.69)			
LNPOP65		−0.03			0.20
		(0.94)			(0.55)
LNNUMPENS			0.299	2.18**	
			(0.59)	(0.00)	
$LNPENCOST_{t-1}$			0.748**		0.33*
			(0.00)		(0.03)
Constant	−27.83**	−27.61**	−1.607	−19.64**	−18.85**
	(0.00)	(0.00)	(0.79)	(0.00)	(0.00)
Adjusted R-squared	0.97	0.97	0.83	0.64	0.97
Durbin-Watson stat	1.37	1.37	2.10	0.98	1.68
F-statistic	405.88	317.36	18.37	9.52	321.42
Observations	49	49	20	20	48

Notes Values in parenthesis are p-value—sample period from 1971 to 2020
Ln denotes all series have been transformed into natural logarithm
** and * denote 1% and 5% levels of significance, respectively

of 20 (Model 3, 4, 5, and 6), *Model 6 is* an adequate model for dependent variable pension cost to OPEX.

Table 2.6 summarises the significant variables that are supported for each dependent variable. The models support all three dependent variables: pension cost, OPEX, and pension cost to OPEX. The only variables that explain the dependent variables are pension cost, life expectancy, and number of pensioners. For OPEX, emoluments and the number of pensioners are two essential variables.

The ratio between pension cost and OPEX has shown a new finding. The finding supports the idea that if GNP increases, the pension cost ratio to OPEX becomes relatively small. Population above 65 years old has a significant impact on the ratio. The number of pensioners is significant in

Table 2.4 Dependent variable 2: Operating expenditure

Independent Variable	*(1)*	*(2)*	*(3)*	*(4)*
Inflation	0.0007	0.002	0.074	0.063
	(0.68)	(0.89)	(0.25)	(0.16)
Crisis	−0.056	−0.040	0.38	−0.001
	(0.63)	(0.72)	(0.138)	(0.99)
LNEMOL	0.42*	0.36*		
	(0.01)	(0.01)		
POP_GR	0.10			
	(0.43)			
LNNUMPENS			1.45**	0.23
			(0.00)	(0.53)
$LNOPEX_{t-1}$	0.58**	0.60**		0.76**
	(0.00)	(0.00)		(0.00)
Constant	0.33	0.176	−7.65	−0.26
	(0.69)	(0.66)	(0.08)	(0.94)
R-squared	0.96	0.9736	0.61	0.82
Durbin-Watson stat	1.85	1.3735	1.11	2.17
F-statistic	204.43	317.36	8.50	17.63
Observations	48	48	20	20

Notes Values in parenthesis are p-value—sample period from 1971 to 2019
Ln denotes all series that have been transformed into natural logarithms.
** and * denote 1% and 5% levels of significance, respectively

all three models. This finding shows that the number of pensioners is the most critical determinant of pension cost.

Table 2.5 Dependent variable: Pension cost over operating expenditure

Independent Variable	*Model*					
	(1)	*(2)*	*(3)*	*(4)*	*(5)*	*(6)*
Inflation	0.035	0.049	−0.14	−0.086	−0.11	0.087
	(0.61)	(0.41)	(0.39)	(0.56)	(0.47)	(0.60)
Crisis	−0.21	−0.20	−1.00	−0.70	−0.90	−0.50
	(0.63)	(0.61)	(0.13)	(0.25)	(0.15)	(0.39)
LIFEXP	1.35*	2.29**			−0.94	2.42
	(0.04)	(0.00)			(0.10)	(0.16)
LNEMOL	−4.14**	−5.78**		−1.84*		
	(0.00)	(0.00)		(0.04)		
LNGNP	2.19					−7.16*
	(0.09)					(0.04)
LNPOP65		4.57**				
		(0.00)				
LNNUMPENS			4.91**	8.90**	9.13**	8.23**
			(0.00)	(0.00)	(0.00)	(0.00)
Constant	−78.15**	−136.20**	−56.56**	−89.83**	−42.15**	−184.47*
	(0.02)	(0.00)	(0.00)	(0.00)	(0.00)	(0.02)
R-squared	0.78	0.81	0.74	0.80	0.78	0.84
Durbin-Watson stat	0.56	0.74	1.03	1.73	1.57	2.00
F-statistic	30.87	36.94	14.83	15.05	13.28	14.17
Observations	49	49	20	20	20	20

Notes Values in parenthesis are p-value—sample period from 1971 to 2019
Ln denotes all series that have been transformed into natural logarithms.
** and * denote 1% and 5% levels of significance, respectively

Table 2.6 Summary of hypothesis test

Hypothesis	*Independent variable (Expected sign)*	*Pension cost*	*OPEX*	*Pension cost to OPEX*
1	Inflation (+)	–	–	-
2	Crisis (-)	–	–	-
3	Life Expectancy (+)	*Supported*	–	*Supported*
4	Emolument (+)	–	*Supported*	*Supported (-)**
5	Population 65 (+)	–	–	*Supported*
6	No. of Pensioners (+)	*Supported*	*Supported*	*Supported*
7	Population Growth (+)	–	–	–
8	GNP (+)	–	–	*Supported (-)***

* When emolument increases, the pension cost to OPEX ratio becomes relatively small. Hence, the negative sign

** When GNP increases, the pension cost to OPEX ratio becomes relatively small. Thus, the negative sign

2.4 Conclusion

The rapidly increasing pattern of pension costs in Malaysia is a severe concern for policymakers and decision-makers. This trend has brought a debate about whether Malaysia needs a pension system reform soon since underfunded public pension systems represent a potential threat to fiscal soundness and, more broadly, economic stability and political risk (Holzmann, 2000).

The pension policy goals promote old-age security, develop a robust capital market, and encourage domestic investment. However, those goals often conflict, especially in developing countries (Orszag & Stiglitz, 2001). This study proves that the number of pensioners is the most critical determinant of the pension cost. Besides, life expectancy will pose a longevity risk to the government's fiscal space.

As shown in the findings, the ratio of pension cost to OPEX will be reduced if the size of the Malaysian economy is enlarged. Hence, the Gross National Product (GNP) expansion is an alternative perspective. With the number of civil servants, the economy should be further enhanced. In other words, the national growth rate must exceed the growth rate of public servants for long-term sustainability. It implies that public servants must serve to facilitate the growth rate and reduce the red tape and bureaucratic processes like the Malaysia Incorporated Policy in the 1980s. In this respect, Public–Private Partnerships must also be intensified. Ultimately, higher GNP will benefit everyone in the nation. It will translate into a higher income and higher welfare for the people.

References

Abas, A. (2019, April 30). Government to reduce number of public service Jobs by 5%. *New Strait Times (NST).* https://www.nst.com.my/news/government-public-policy/2019/04/484308/171-million-civil-servants-govt-payroll-march-2019

Abd Manaf, N. H. (2011). Public administration in Southeast Asia. *Taylor and Francis Group, 309–309.* https://doi.org/10.4135/9781452283241.n50

Abdul Rahman, M. I., & Lau, W.Y. (2023). Is the KWAP defined benefit pension fund sustainable in the long run? *International Journal of Banking and Finance, 18*(2), 97–126. https://doi.org/10.32890/ijbf2023.18.2.5

Barr, N., & Diamond, P. (2006). The economics of pensions. *Oxford Review of Economic Policy, 22*(1), 15–39. https://doi.org/10.1093/oxrep/grj002

Chee, L. K. (1997). The Malaysian government pension scheme. Whither its future direction ? *Jurnal Ekonomi Malaysia, 31*, 87–106.

Clark, G. L., & Hebb, T. (2003). Understanding pension fund corporate engagement in a global arena. *SASE Conference Paper,* https://www.Sase.Org/Conf2003/Papers/Clark-Hebb.Pdf

Clark, R. L., Craig, L. A., & Wilson, J. W. (2003). *Pension economics*. University of Pennsylvania Press

Clark, R. L., & McDermed, A. A. (1990). *The choice of pension plans in a changing regulatory environment*. Books.

Davis, E. P. (2005). *The role of pension funds as institutional investors in emerging markets.*

Davis, E. P., & Hu, Y.-W. (2004). *Is there a Link Between pension-fund Assets and Economic Growth?-A Cross-Country Study? Public Policy Discussion Papers 04–23.* School of Social Sciences, Brunel University.

Disney, R. (2003). Are contributions to public pension programmes a tax? *Fourth Annual CeRP Conference, Turin, 16.*

DOSM. (2018). Department of statistics Malaysia press release. *Department of Statistics Malaysia, 2018*(September), 5–9. https://doi.org/10.1017/CBO9781107415324.004

Gustman, A. L., & Steinmeier, T. L. (1992). The stampede toward defined contribution pension plans: Fact or fiction? *Industrial Relations: A Journal of Economy and Society, 31*(2), 361–369.

Holzmann, R. (2000). The World Bank Approach to Pension Reform. *International Social Security Review, 53*(1), 11–34.

Holzmann, R., & Hinz, R. (2005). Old-Age income support in the 21st Century. In *Old-Age Income Support in the 21st Century* (Issue January 2005). https://doi.org/10.1596/0-8213-6040-x

Hussein, N. (2019). The Malaysian pension system. *Nomura Foundation*, 15–20. http://www.nomurafoundation.or.jp/en/wordpress/wp-content/uploads/2019/03/NJACM3-2SP19-04.pdf

Ibrahim, R. I. (2012). Impact of increasing retirement age on longevity factor: An empirical study for government pensioners in Malaysia. *Jurnal Ekonomi Malaysia, 46*(2), 29–35.

Lee, K. C. (1997). The Malaysian government ppension scheme. Whither is its future direction? *Jurnal Ekonomi Malaysia, 31*, 87–106.

Lindell, C. (2003). Finnish Centre for Pensions Working Papers 6 Longevity is increasing—what about the retirement age ? Finnish Centre for Pensions Working Papers 6 Longevity is increasing – what about the retirement age ? At the *4th International Research Conference on Social Security in Antwerp*.

Machnes, Y. (2000). *Increasing life expectancy and reforms in pension plans*. Bar-Ilan University, Ramat-Gan, Israel.

Martell, C. R., Kioko, S. N., & Moldogaziev, T. (2013). Impact of unfunded pension obligations on credit quality of state governments. *Public Budgeting and Finance, 33*(3), 24–54. https://doi.org/10.1111/j.1540-5850.2013.12013.x

MOF. (2020). *Estimated Federal Expenditure 2021*. http://belanjawan2021.treasury.gov.my/index.php/en/ap-2021

MOF, M. of F. (2019). Malaysia 2020 Budget Speech by YB Tuan Lim Guan Eng. *Parliament Malaysia*, *October 2019*, 1–13.

Moore, R. L. (1987). Are male/female earnings differentials related to life-expectancy-caused pension cost differences? *Economic Inquiry, 25*(3), 389–401.

Munnell, A. H., Aubry, J. P., & Quinby, L. (2011). Public pension funding in practice. *Journal of Pension Economics and Finance, 10*(2), 247–268. https://doi.org/10.1017/S1474747211000126

Orszag, P. R., & Stiglitz, J. E. (2001). Rethinking pension reform: Ten Myths about social security systems. *New Ideas about Old Age Security*, 17–56.

Retirement Fund Act 2007 (*Act 662*).(2007) *Malaysia*, *December*. www.iicm.org.my/wp-content/uploads/2019/04/KWAp-Compliance-with-II-Code-31-Dec-2018.pdf

Roy, A. (2012). Innovative approaches to managing longevity risk in Asia: Lessons from the West. *ADB Working Paper*, *353*. https://doi.org/10.2139/ssrn.2039236

The World Bank. (2008). The World Bank pension conceptual framework. *World Bank Pension Reform Primer*, *202*, 8. http://hdl.handle.net/10986/11139

United Nations, D. of E. A. S. D. and P. (2019). *World Mortality 2019*. 24.

Walker, E., & Lefort, F. (2000). *Pension reform and capital markets: Are there any (Hard) Links?* Available at SSRN 239531.

Yew, S. Y., & Cheong, K. C. (2013). Ageing and the economic welfare of Southeast Asian Nations. *Malaysian Journal of Economic Studies, 50*(2), 101–106.

CHAPTER 3

Asset Allocation and Performance

3.1 Introduction

The Malaysian government has admitted that paying pensions has become a significant financial burden. Pension payments are expected to reach around RM47 billion in 2030 compared to RM28 billion in 2022, a 67% increase within eight years (Daim & Yunus, 2021).

In addition, a recent court of appeals' decision declaring the modified Pensions Adjustment Act unconstitutional, which took effect in January 2013, represents the worst-case scenario for the Malaysian government (FMT, 2022). This court decision saddled the government with a vast pension problem that could cost billions of Ringgit in Malaysia backdated claims (Parkaran, 2022).

The issue emerged when the government revised civil servants' salaries in 2013 and offered retirees who took their retirement after the change a bigger pension and a 2% annual raise. For people who retired before 2013, however, their pension payment was still based on their pre-retirement pay plus a 2% yearly raise. Because a new pension plan cannot be less beneficial than an existing one, the modified statute violated Article 147 of the Federal Constitution (Anbalagan, 2022).

Regardless of the pending court cases, the Malaysian government still has to bear a high pension obligation. The Malaysian government is adjusting a new civil service retirement plan to protect employees' well-being while optimising long-term government spending.

M. I. Abdul Rahman and W. Y. Lau, *Pension at Stake*,
https://doi.org/10.1007/978-981-97-2324-9_3

Hence, the Malaysian government is more pressured to manage its pension fund to meet higher obligations in the future. In the case of defined benefit plans for Malaysian civil servants, the goal of the investment function is to generate the highest possible returns consistent with the future liabilities requirement. Furthermore, managing the assets for pension funds is crucial since it reflects the pension fund's performance in the near and long term.

Retirement Fund Incorporated (KWAP)

Parliament of Malaysia enacted the Retirement Fund Act 2007 (Act 662) in March 2007 to establish a new statutory body named Retirement Fund (Incorporated). The act replaces the abolished Pensions Trust Fund Act of 1991 (Act 454), designed to help the federal government meet its pension obligations. This retirement fund (Incorporated), known as "Kumpulan Wang Persaraan (Diperbadankan)" (KWAP), was launched as a capital start-up of RM500 million (KWAP, 2007).

KWAP is a statutory body governed by the Ministry of Finance that manages the pension scheme for Malaysia's public employees. KWAP is a fund manager for the Malaysia public pension fund for financing the government's future liability and responsibility for administering and paying pensions to public sector retirees.

As Government-Linked Investment Companies (GLIC), KWAP is one of the three central bodies managing Malaysia's pension scheme besides EPF and LTAT. In 2015, KWAP took over the Post-Pension Services Division of the Public Services Department (PSD). It oversees the distribution of pensions, gratuities, and other benefits the Malaysian government provides (KWAP, 2017).

With the incorporation of KWAP, all of the Pensions Trust Fund's authorities, functions, activities, assets, and liabilities were transferred to KWAP. KWAP aims to administer the retirement fund (the Fund) established by Section 3 of the Retirement Fund Act 2007 (Act 662) to maximise returns through benchmarking, a flexible investment strategy, and responsible for prudence risk management. The Fund will help finance the Federal government's pension obligation in the future.

Since KWAP has operated for 12 years, the total fund size at cost has increased. In 2007, the total fund at cost was recorded at RM47.42 billion, reaching the highest fund, RM141 billion, in 2017, before it went down to RM137 billion in 2018. The year under review saw the full adoption of Malaysian Financial Reporting Standards (MFRS) 9, which replaced the previous MFRS 139 (KWAP, 2018).

Table 3.1 shows that the gross income of KWAP rose to a record of RM 9.03 billion ($2.32 billion) in 2017 on the back of a 5.77% return on investment. The total fund size expanded to RM 140.8 billion from RM 125 billion a year earlier.

KWAP has full responsibility for investing and managing the respective fund. Any KWAP's new investments must follow policies the investment panel sets, with the board's approval. These include a strategic asset allocation, which needs to be reviewed periodically to assure optimal returns from relatively low-risk investments.

The Investment Policy and Guidelines govern all KWAP's investing activities. However, the investment panel and the board will receive regular reports on the status and performance of KWAP's assets. As a sole fund manager for the government, assessing KWAP's performance and strategies is essential to ensure the government's financial sustainability in paying the pension and future obligations.

Creating and balancing the pension portfolio entails managing asset allocation for each asset class. After all, it is one of the critical factors in determining portfolio returns. Selecting the ideal stocks, bonds, cash, and real estate asset mix for the portfolio is fluid. The asset mix should, therefore, constantly reflect the investing objectives. This study intends to examine KWAP's asset allocation as part of its investment strategy. Does KWAP's asset allocation strategy yield the best return after all? This chapter intends to answer this question.

Asset and Liability Management in Pension Funds

Managing pension funds is not as forward as it is. The pension fund around the globe is sometimes more significant than some countries' GDP. Preliminary data by the OECD (2020) report shows the total pension fund assets of up to USD 30 trillion held by seven OECD countries: the United Kingdom, the United States of America, Australia, Netherlands, Canada, Japan, and Switzerland.

A pension fund cannot just maximise its returns using the traditional efficient method. Chernoff (2003) explained that one way to manage a pension fund is by matching pension assets against pension liabilities. However, besides providing pension liabilities to the pensioners,

Table 3.1 Snapshot of KWAP performance 2007–2018

Year 20XX	*2007*	*2008*	*2009*	*2010*	*2011*	*2012*	*2013*	*2014*	*2015*	*2016*	*2017*	*2018*
Fund Size	48.08	52.04	61.5	70.52	78.93	88.73	99.92	109.43	118.37	125	140.8	136.51
Gross Invt Income	3.75	3.01	3.24	4.62	4.66	5.75	6.66	6.47	6.40	6.40	9.00	7.06
Net Income	3.67	0.56	5.70	4.85	4.30	5.69	6.57	4.84	4.40	4.80	8.80	1.20
Gross ROI(%)	9.21%	5.86%	5.62%	7.07%	6.30%	6.84%	7.05%	6.15%	5.40%	5.40%	5.80%	4.10%
Net ROI(%)	9.79%	1.12%	10.04%	7.34%	5.75%	6.79%	6.97%	4.58%	3.26%	4.00%	7.00%	0.80%

Note Fund Size is measured in RM Billion, Gross Invt Income (Gross Investment Income) is measured in RM Billion, Net Income is measured in RM Billion, Gross Return on Investment (%) and Net Return on Investment (%)
Source KWAP Financial Report

Ito (1995) argues that pension fund sponsors have a secondary goal to achieve an "earning spread" to reduce the future liabilities requirement.

For example, the Malaysia pension funds have been previously studied by Jidwin et al. (2012) in a fund selection, performance, and perception survey. The study results reveal that members' experiences of investment performances were mixed. Meeting a guaranteed minimum return to the contributors as a pension fund manager is challenging.

The Choice Between Asset Classes

An asset class is a group of assets with similar investment characteristics. Each asset class will carry various risk factors, such as equity market risk, interest rates, inflation, or currency risk. Thus controlling, asset class weights control the portfolio's risk exposures.

The literature suggested that a debate on optimal asset allocation has two extreme views. According to one viewpoint, bonds are the sole option to align assets with liabilities. At the same time, another perspective advises that the assets must have equity exposure. A pension fund's main potential asset classes are presented in this section, including fixed income, equity, money market, and investing in alternative investments such as real estate, private equity, and commodities. Traditionally, equity and fixed income are the main asset classes in pension funds, whereas alternative investment is growing in demand.

For example, the OECD (2020) report shows that OECD pension funds were primarily invested in equities and fixed-income asset classes. Out of 36 OECD countries, 16 held more than 75% of their pension portfolios in equities and bonds. However, Papke (1991) finds the asset allocation of US private pension funds where the percentage holds fixed income and equities different by the type of employer. Single-employer plans tend to have about 60% fixed-income securities and another 20% equity securities. The smaller single employers invest 50% and 20%, respectively. They found that equity allocation increased its share from 48% in 1991 to 57% in 2001. Differently, Blake et al. (1999) found that 300 UK pension funds have a higher percentage allocation to equities than fixed-income securities. However, this study concentrates on pension performance rather than asset allocation.

The reason to invest in each class for pension funds is discussed below:

Fixed Income

The main idea behind investing in fixed-income securities is to match assets and liabilities. Theoretically, a fully funded pension fund with a financially stable sponsor, such as a government backup, should not take an additional risk by investing in equity. According to Blake (2001), regulators encouraged fixed income since the bond yields were a reference for actuaries and accountants to calculate pension liability. This feature is why fixed income is one of the securities that can avoid any short-term mismatch between assets and future liabilities. As a result, the asset allocation of pension funds should be more heavily weighted towards bonds.

Equity

Despite what some managers think about fixed-income securities as the only way to hedge pension liabilities, Black (1989) finds that stocks or equity securities can achieve higher expected returns in a portfolio. Higher returns will lower expected liability costs in the future. Even stocks should be viewed as inflation-protected as stock prices and the expected rate of inflation move in tandem. Similarly, Chun et al. (2000) research that any growing company typically should have more concentration on equity and lower allocation on bonds or real estate due to a higher expected rate of return.

Money Market and Cash Equivalent

Despite the literature suggesting a fixed income and equity exposure, investing in the money market asset class is important. The sponsor has to keep cash in the form of cash equivalent for liquidity requirement purposes. Any short-term debt instruments such as Treasury Bills, Fixed Deposits, and Commercial Paper are part of the money market instrument. KWAP does not allow its members to withdraw some savings before retirement age.

Alternative Investment

Real estate is part of the alternative investment asset classes. Malaysian pension funds have traditionally held less real estate in their portfolio. Many researchers have found that real estate is great for capital preservation but has a moderate rate of return. Hudson-Wilson et al. (2005) explain that real estate is essential to define benefit pension funds to hedge inflation through benefit payments that happen in real terms.

For example, Chun et al. (2000) discovered little correlation between US pension fund real estate allocation and pension plan obligations. The primary role of real estate is to hedge against inflation risk.

Strategic Asset Allocation and Tactical Asset Allocation

A comprehensive asset allocation method that considers the long-term and strategically optimal fund allocation across asset classes has been used to guide investment decisions. The Strategic Asset Allocation (SAA) is typically based on each asset type's risk and return characteristics. Different levels of risk will result from different potential asset allocations. Since it establishes most of the risk associated with its investments, it is a crucial step in the investment process.

An optimal asset allocation is a process in which the sponsor weighs the asset allocation dynamically. The SAA is the highest level of decision-making in the investment process. Hence, Alestalo and Puttonen (2006) discuss pension fund portfolio management in two steps.

The first step is where the sponsor company must identify which broad asset classes to invest in strategic asset allocation. These asset classes include but are not limited to fixed income, equity, money market instruments, real estate, private equity, or even commodities. This step will significantly impact how well a pension fund performs.

The second is asset allocation implementation via internal or external fund managers. This step is critical when choosing the right fund managers based on their investment strategies or security selection process. The sponsor should consider a fund manager with a higher information ratio, indicating additional alpha over additional unit risk.

Besides SAA, Tactical Asset Allocation (TAA) is another choice made during the investment process, allowing the fund manager to deviate from the asset allocation budgeted in the SAA. TAA entails making short-term deviations from the SAA to profit from mispricing in the capital markets.

After all, a pension fund's ideal asset mix depends on many factors. Those factors cover regulation and compliance, the market view for future liability, the sponsor's ability to take the risk, and the funded status. Hence, defining an optimal asset allocation is difficult, given the complexity of those factors.

Sharpe Ratio and M2 Risk-Adjusted Performance Measurement

The Sharpe Ratio is widely applied in the financial sector. Fund managers frequently use the Sharpe Ratio to prove their expertise and skill. On the other hand, Leah and Franco (1997) recommended employing a risk-adjusted performance approach, where each portfolio is adjusted to the degree of risk in its unmanaged benchmark before the performance of this risk-equivalent portfolio is measured. This ratio is known as the M2 ratio, this performance ratio recognises that the risk of a portfolio can be readily altered and provides the basis for an actual result of risk-adjusted performance.

Modern Portfolio Theory (MPT) and Its Application

Harry Markowitz published his doctoral thesis in 1954. His thesis later became the foundation of the Modern Portfolio Theory (MPT). The thesis changed the way people viewed risk and showed that in a portfolio context, the risk that is important to the investor is not the total volatility of individual security in the portfolio but rather how the securities correlate with each other in such a way as cancel out some of these risks.

Until Markowitz, investors did not consider the risk of a security in the context of a portfolio. Each security would be gauged on its risks, and securities with higher volatility would be penalised more heavily.

Efficient Frontier

The Global Market Portfolio can be used as a baseline portfolio for asset allocation. The point contains all risky investable assets, eliminating all diversifiable risks. As a starting point, the biases of an individual client (or manager) are mitigated. The weights by asset classes can then be lifted to meet the objectives of a given client.

The efficient frontier graph collects the best risk for a given level of expected return or the best return for a given level of expected risk. Portfolios below the efficient frontier are considered suboptimal portfolios—where these portfolios do not provide sufficient return for their level of risk.

For example, Abu Bakar and Rosbi (2018) studied efficient frontier analysis for portfolio investment in the Malaysian stock market. Tunaru et al. (2006) looked at the Chinese Stock market. Both studies found the efficient frontier application to determine the optimal weight for securities in a portfolio.

The dots represent the risk and return of the different combinations of investment assets. It is possible to draw a curve that defines the outer boundary of these dots. The curve is called the efficient frontier. After all, it represents that the different combinations of efficient portfolios along this line are "efficient" because they give one the highest return for a given level of risk and the lowest risk for a given level of return.

Portfolios below the efficient frontier are inefficient because one can achieve a more efficient portfolio (with higher return or lower risk) by choosing one that lies on the efficient frontier. Take, for instance, Portfolio A. It is an inefficient portfolio because one can invest in Portfolio B, which gives one a higher return for the same risk, or Portfolio C, which offers a lower risk for the same return. A portfolio that lies above the efficient frontier is not achievable because the efficient frontier already represents the best possible combination of risk and return that the fund manager can achieve.

The investor's objective is to find a portfolio that lies on this efficient frontier because this portfolio gives one the best risk/return combination. MPT tells one how investors can combine the various asset classes. For example, rather than choosing a portfolio that is 100% bonds, MPT shows that one can achieve more efficient portfolios. The investors can achieve higher returns and the same risk by having 50% bonds and 50% equities in the portfolio or higher returns and lower risk by having 75% and 25% equities.

Capital Asset Pricing Model (CAPM)

The CAPM, formulated by Sharpe, Lintner, and Mossin, enhances the returns achievable from relying on the efficient frontier. The risk-free asset would be added to the efficient frontier, and the investors can effectively be extended to the efficient frontier. Hence, to make this possible, the investors must be able to invest some portion in a risk-free asset, such as cash deposits, or borrow at the risk-free rate to buy a larger amount of investment assets.

The optimal combination of portfolios with the best risk/return trade-off is no longer the efficient frontier when investors do this. Instead, a straight line called the Capital Market Line (CML) starts at the risk-free asset return rate and runs tangent to the efficient frontier.

Under the CAPM, the only portfolio the investor should hold in combination with the risk-free asset is the Market Portfolio, which is the portfolio at the tangency between the CML and the efficient frontier.

As CAPM defines, the Market Portfolio contains all risky assets globally, including bonds, shares, gold, and stamps. However, as it is impossible to identify these assets in practice, the Market Portfolio is a widely diversified portfolio of Malaysian and international equities and bonds.

The CML is a straight line starting at the risk-free asset return and tangent to the efficient frontier. The Market Portfolio (m) is the portfolio that lies in the tangency between the CML and the efficient frontier.

The slope of CML represents the price the market is willing to pay for the risk of the efficient portfolio. It is the additional return that the market requires for each percentage increase in the portfolio risk—standard deviation of returns—and is calculated as Eq. (3.1) as below:

$$E(r_n) = r_f + \frac{E(r_m) - r_f}{\sigma_m}\sigma_p. \tag{3.1}$$

In different words, Eq. (3.2) is as follows:

$$E(r_n) = r_f + \beta_p\left[E(r_m) - r_f\right]. \tag{3.2}$$

where $E(r_n)$ denotes the expected additional return that the market requires for each percentage increase in the portfolio risk, r_f denotes a risk-free rate, β_p denotes the portfolio beta, and $E(r_m)$ is expected market return.

3.2 Methodology

This study uses secondary data from KWAP financial reports from 2007 to 2018. The goal is to study its asset allocation precisely and pension fund performance since the KWAP was founded.

Gross Investment (GI) Income per Basis Point (bps)

Based on an annual KWAP gross investment income from 2007 to 2018, this study computes gross income per 1 bps. A basis point (bps) is a standard measure for interest rates and finance percentage, representing one-hundredth per cent. Equation (3.3) for each gross investment income per 1bps for year t and security i is as below:

$$GI\ per\ bps_{t,i} = \frac{\text{Gross Investment Income}_{t,i}}{\text{Percentage of Asset Allocated}_{t,i}}. \tag{3.3}$$

The idea is to measure how asset allocation for each 1bps decision impacted the total gross investment income, see which assets also contributed the most for the past eleven years, and see which asset class contributed the most and the least. This calculation is based on the average gross investment income over the average percentage for each institution's asset allocation. However, this calculation may ignore the fund manager's competence and the scenario assumptions (economic cycle).

Portfolio Performance

Performance measurement for the KWAP portfolio can be measured. However, due to the limited information on the pension providers, only two ratios are commonly used in performance evaluation able to generate:

First, the Sharpe Ratio represents the slope of the CML. A higher ratio means a better asset. Equations (3.4) and (3.5) are defined as the portfolio risk premium dividend by the portfolio risk:

$$\text{Sharpe Ratio} = \frac{\text{Market Risk Premium(MRP)}}{\sigma_P}. \tag{3.4}$$

$$\text{Sharpe Ratio} = \frac{R_P - R_F}{\sigma_P}. \tag{3.5}$$

The second ratio is the M2 ratio—an extension of the Sharpe Ratio that provides the investors with the risk-adjusted return to the portfolio by multiplying the Sharpe Ratio with the standard deviation of any benchmark market index and adding a risk-free return. Equations (3.6), (3.7),

Table 3.2 Variables for Sharpe Ratio and M2 Ratio

Item	*Details*	*Variables*	*Source*
R_P	Return Premium	Represented by Return on Investment (ROI)	KWAP
R_f	Risk-Free Rate	Represented by one-year Treasury Bills	Bloomberg
σ_P	Portfolio Standard Deviation	Represented by Portfolio Volatility	KWAP
σ_m	Market Standard Deviation	Represented by Volatility of Stock Price Index for Malaysia (KLSE)	FRED Economic Research

The Market Standard Deviation retrieved from Bank (2021)

and (3.8) are shown as follows:

$$M^2 = \left[(\text{Market Risk Premium (MRP)}) \times \frac{\sigma_m}{\sigma_p}\right] + R_f. \quad (3.6)$$

$$M^2 = \left[\left(R_P - R_f\right) \times \frac{\sigma_m}{\sigma_p}\right] + R_f. \quad (3.7)$$

$$M^2 = \left[\text{Sharpe Ratio} \times \sigma_m\right] + R_f. \quad (3.8)$$

Table 3.2 shows variables to compute a fund performance ratio, Sharpe Ratio, and M2 Risk-Adjusted Performance ratio.

Efficient Frontier and Capital Market Line (CML)

Using the data from January 2007 to December 2020, this study computes the efficient frontier of the investment based on Markowitz's Theory with asset classes listed in Table 3.3.

Table 3.3 shows five asset classes to be used in computing efficient frontier. For every asset class, a proxy has determined to see the return for each asset class. The main objective of this exercise is to develop a supported modern portfolio theory. Modern portfolio theory seeks the collection of all portfolios that constitute the efficient frontier. The efficient collection comprises all portfolios between the efficient frontier's maximum return portfolio and the global minimum variance portfolio. The portfolio on the efficient frontier with the lowest risk is the smallest

Table 3.3 Asset classes proxy variable in computing efficient frontier

Asset class	*Variables*	*Source*
Domestic equity	Represented by Kuala Lumpur Stock Exchange (KLSE)	Bloomberg
Fixed income	Represented by S&P Malaysia Total Bond Return	Bloomberg
Money market	A proxy for short-term Ringgit Malaysia money market instrument. Represented by Kuala Lumpur Inter-Bank Offer Rate (KLIBOR). One-month KLIBOR is used	Bloomberg
Real estate	Represented by Bursa Malaysia Property Index	Bloomberg
International stocks	Represented by MSCI World Index. A proxy for all international stocks and exposures	Bloomberg

variance portfolio; the portfolio on the efficient frontier with the highest projected return might be the highest return portfolio. No other portfolio within the opportunity set has an equal or larger return but lower risk. However, the utmost return portfolio has the lowest risk on the efficient frontier

Based on the efficient frontier, this study tries to identify the ideal investment weighting to maximise return while minimising investment risk. According to Markowitz's Theory, the investment risk is minimised by utilising a mix of stocks and securities. Therefore, this study performed statistical diagnostics to find the mean, standard deviation, and correlation for different asset classes. Furthermore, using an effective frontier approach, the Markowitz equation incorporates these three variables to determine the weight to lower portfolio risk.

3.3 Results and Discussion

KWAP ROI, Asset Allocation, and Gross Investment

This study examines the asset allocation pattern from 2007 to 2018 by KWAP.

In the latest financial report, KWAP (2018) allocated approximately 46% of its investment assets to fixed-income instruments, 40% to equity securities, and 14% to private equity and real estate, referring to alternative investments. Most of KWAP's investments are in Malaysia, and international portfolio assets account for approximately 13% of its investment assets.

Return on Investment (ROI)

Figure 3.1 shows the KWAP ROI from 2007 to 2018. KWAP was initiated in 2007 and had a drop-in return in the second year, about 6%, when recorded at 9% in the first year. The effect of crises can be observed throughout these eleven years, from the poor performance of the KWAP fund from 2007 to 2008. The US and UK stock markets underperformed throughout the Subprime and European crises in 2008 and 2009, contributing to the low returns in these years. Since Malaysia's preferred international capital markets were the US and the UK, this had a significant impact and might affect our worldwide investors and return.

KWAP Asset Classes

Figure 3.2 shows that KWAP has invested in four main asset classes since its inception: equity, fixed income, money market, and real estate. In 2007, KWAP started its asset allocation of about 48% in a fixed-income

Fig. 3.1 KWAP Return on Investment (ROI) from 2007 to 2018 (*Source* KWAP Annual Financial Report)

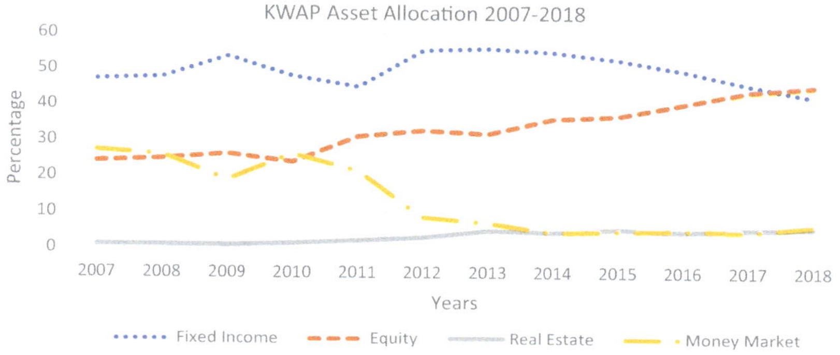

Fig. 3.2 KWAP asset allocation 2007–2018 (*Source* KWAP Annual Financial Report)

portfolio, 24% in equity, and 27% in money market placement. The fixed-income portfolio and money market have been reduced throughout the eleven years, while equity and real estate have gradually increased.

Regarding equity allocation, KWAP has had a rising trend in investing its funds into equity investment since the beginning. Hence, it explained that KWAP had been a substantial shareholder among Malaysia's largest listed companies (KWAP, 2019). The companies include Tenaga Nasional and the top two financial institutions: Malayan Banking (Maybank) and CIMB Group Holdings (CIMB). Any dividend-paying sector, such as banking and telecommunications, is favoured by KWAP.

The Society of Actuaries SOA (2011) elaborated that many pension plans continue to invest in equity securities by taking additional risks. However, financial economists would argue that liabilities are bond-like and plan assets would be best placed in high-quality (or risk-free) fixed-income investments. However, the sponsor must realise where the fund will be susceptible to down market cycles and equity market volatility compared to fixed income. Regarding fixed income, KWAP has been reduced from 47% of its investment fund in 2007 to 42.31% in 2018. The 10% reduction over eleven years shows that KWAP has increased its risk tolerance since its initiation.

In the early ages of KWAP, higher allocation to the money market asset classes was up to 26% to 27% for the first four years (2007–2010). Since KWAP has less liquidity requirement, the exposure on money market assets should be lower since it generates a lower return than other asset classes.

KWAP's allocation into real estate is also on a rising trend. Over the eleven years, KWAP has increased its weight from 1% to 5.6% in real estate by 2018. According to Hudson-Wilson et al. (2005), real estate has acquired acceptability as a mainstream asset class among institutional investors. High capital flows, high prices, reduced yields, and expansion of the real estate universe into relatively untested property kinds or international markets are all issues with this acceptance.

Gross Investment Income

This study computes each asset class's average gross investment income over average allocation for eleven years (2007–2018). Table 3.4 shows the gross investment income for each 1% allocation by asset classes. On average, the real estate asset has demonstrated the highest performing asset classes within eleven years, contributing about RM100 million per one per cent. This number contributed to high performance for real estate in 2013 and 2014 (Abdul Rahman and Lau, 2023; Irfan and Lau, 2024).

Investing in equity is the second-highest asset class, contributing to KWAP's gross investment income. On average, equity investment contributed about RM80 million per one per cent allocation. However, investing in equities or stocks contributed the highest income for every year except 2013 and 2014. Furthermore, investing in fixed income contributed an average of RM50 million and money market placement of RM30 million per one per cent. The recent year of 2018 saw the fixed income contribute the highest income per 1bps compared to other asset classes.

Performance Ratio for KWAP 2009–2018

Table 3.5 shows that KWAP's asset performance has been accessed into two different performance ratios from 2009 to 2018 using i) Sharpe Ratio and ii) M^2 risk-adjusted performance. This study uses the Sharpe Ratio to measure portfolio return earned a year above the risk-free rate per unit of risk the plans take. Portfolio volatility is measured by changes in an asset or portfolio's price fluctuations. Hence, the risk-adjusted performance of a portfolio is determined by its Sharpe Ratio. As a result, the higher the

Table 3.4 Gross investment income for each 1% by asset class

Years	*KWAP gross income per 100bps*			
	Equity (MYR Billion)	*Fixed income (MYR Billion)*	*Money market (MYR Billion)*	*Real estate (MYR Billion)*
2007	0.10(1)	0.02(3)	0.01(4)	0.06(2)
2008	0.05(1)	0.02(3)	0.02(4)	0.03(2)
2009	0.05(1)	0.03(3)	0.02(4)	0.04(2)
2010	0.10(1)	0.04(3)	0.01(4)	0.04(2)
2011	0.07(1)	0.04(3)	0.02(4)	0.04(2)
2012	0.09(1)	0.04(3)	0.04(4)	0.08(2)
2013	0.07(2)	0.04(3)	0.03(4)	0.36(1)
2014	0.07(2)	0.05(3)	0.04(4)	0.24(1)
2015	0.09(1)	0.05(2)	0.05(3)	0.02(4)
2016	0.07(2)	0.06(3)	0.04(4)	0.10(1)
2017	0.10(2)	0.09(3)	0.03(4)	0.12(1)
2018	0.04(2)	0.11(1)	0.04(4)	0.04(3)
Average	**0.08(2)**	**0.05(3)**	**0.03(4)**	**0.10(1)**

Parentheses The fund ranking between four asset classes within a year
Source Author's computation

Sharpe Ratio, the more appealing the risk-adjusted return above the risk-free rate for any given portfolio.

KWAP recorded the highest ratio in 2010, at 2.22, compared to the previous year 1.33. The number contributed to the highest portfolio return that year, 7.07%, with only 1.9% of volatility. Based on modern portfolio theory, low-correlation assets can be added to a diversified portfolio to lower risk without reducing return. Based on this view, the Sharpe Ratio has emerged as the most popular technique for determining the risk-adjusted return. Hence, lowering risk and increasing

Table 3.5 KWAP's asset performance 2009–2018

Performance ratio (20XX)	*09*	*10*	*11*	*12*	*13*	*14*	*15*	*16*	*17*	*18*
Sharpe Ratio	1.33	2.22	0.92	1.34	1.28	1.12	0.90	0.97	1.21	0.47
M^2	27.5	29.6	11.2	16.9	13.9	12.6	10.7	14.0	12.2	9.16

Source Author's Computation

return should raise the Sharpe Ratio compared to any similar portfolio. A higher diversification level can be interpreted in a high Sharpe Ratio.

The Sharpe Ratio can also tell whether a portfolio's excess returns result from wise investment choices or unreasonably high risk. Although one portfolio or fund can enjoy higher returns than another, it is not considered a wise investment unless reflected in a higher Sharpe Ratio.

KWAP, in 2011, has aggressively taken a higher risk. The highest risk in 2011 contributed to a lower Sharpe Ratio of 0.92 than the previous year's highest. The Sharpe Ratio decreased from 2012 to 2015, increasing risk and reducing the pattern in return. It shows that KWAP has aggressively taken an additional risk that does not contribute to better performance.

Second, this study uses the M2 ratio in evaluating performance. Even the Sharpe Ratio has been interested in assessing the excess return from any risk-free asset over risk. We can interpret the value of the M2 measure as the difference between the scaled excess return of a portfolio and that of the market, where the scaled portfolio has the same volatility as the market. It could imply that the M2 estimate is the return a portfolio would have generated if it had the same level of risk as the index.

The ratio by KWAP has been decreasing since 2007. The trend shows that the KWAP portfolio performs better early since its returns are better considering its risk. The highly diversified M2 metric is a useful tool for portfolio management. It helps to understand the given level of risk assumed in a portfolio where it will reward the investor compared to the benchmark portfolio and risk-free rate of return.

Therefore, if an investment is considered to have more risk than the benchmark, it might have fewer risk-adjusted performances with few benefits. The M^2 measure facilitates the interpretation and helps compare two or more portfolios by the investor.

In conclusion, KWAP's performance has deteriorated for the past ten years. Based on the analysis, KWAP has aggressively taken additional risks without considering any alpha return (above risk-free return) for one unit of risk. Despite the return on investment in a reducing trend, the ratio has contributed to higher market risk.

Global Market Portfolio and Efficient Frontier

Figure 3.3 shows the computer-efficient frontier graph and the Capital Market Line (CML) computed using proxy variables for each asset class.

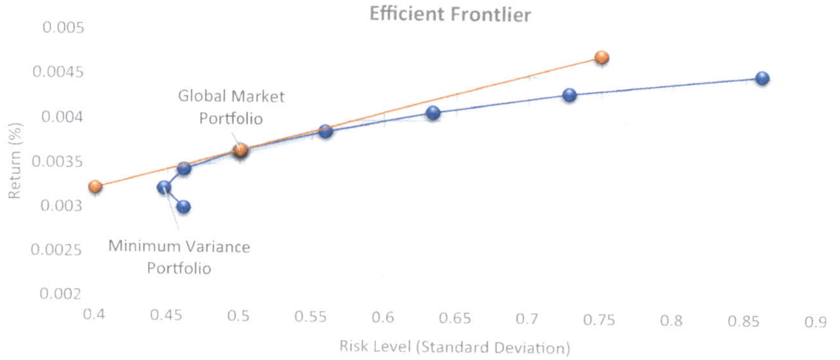

Fig. 3.3 Capital Market Line (CML) and efficient frontier graph (*Source* Author's computation)

The point between these two graphs is the Global Market Portfolio, where the most diversified asset allocation point is in the graph.

The CAL, also called the Capital Market Line (CML), is depicted as a line on a graph representing all possible combinations of risk-free and risky assets. Capital allocation is the allocation of funds between risky and riskless assets. The foremost excellent range of expected returns is frequently attained by combining the portfolio with the best return on the efficient frontier with a riskless asset. Any investor can choose the combination that best suits them regardless of risk aversion.

Table 3.6 shows a correlation between asset classes, as expected that fixed income will negatively correlate with equity exposure (0.191). Real estate and international stock classes have a high correlation with equity classes. When the economy grows, the logic is reflected by higher stock prices, and real estate will boom.

Table 3.7 shows three asset allocation proposals in different situations. A minimum variance portfolio is where asset allocation has the lowest risk-taking compared to its peer portfolio. A diversified portfolio has less risk as compared to another portfolio. The minimum variance portfolio produces almost 20% for each asset class. These three situations are derived from scenario analysis to produce the weightage for each asset.

This point allocation refers to a diversified portfolio that creates the lowest point of volatility. This point in the efficient graph is suitable for risk-averse investors. The philosophy behind risk-averse investors is

Table 3.6 Correlation matrix between asset class

Asset class	*Equity*	*Fixed income*	*Money market*	*Real estate*	*International stocks*
Domestic equity	1.000	0.191	−0.274	0.746	0.607
Fixed income	0.191	1.000	0.057	0.207	0.122
Money market	−0.274	0.057	1.000	−0.205	−0.221
Real estate	0.746	0.207	−0.205	1.000	0.597
International stocks	0.607	0.122	−0.221	0.597	1.000

Source Authors' Computation

Table 3.7 Asset allocation based on efficient frontier graph

Asset class	*Asset allocation*		
	Minimum variance portfolio (%)	*Global market portfolio (%)*	*High risk (%)*
Domestic equity	19.98	17.13	0.00
Fixed income	2003	24.95	15.23
Money market	20.04	12.42	0.00
Real estate	19.97	8.70	0.00
International stocks	19.98	36.80	84.77

Source Authors' computation

to spread the eggs across the baskets. As the share of risky assets in the portfolio grows, so does the risk until the portfolio consists entirely of hazardous assets. The portfolio's risk is the combination of the risk of the assets. Diversification lowers risk by integrating assets with different correlation coefficients among the assets that make up the portfolio. Because all assets are exposed to systemic risk produced by macroeconomic issues that affect almost all assets, most assets have some correlation.

Global Market Portfolio is where asset allocation produces the highest Sharpe Ratio and acts as a baseline for asset allocation. Global Market Portfolio is weighting tilt towards the international stocks or international exposure. An international market has many transactions; investors might eliminate a few liquidities and delay risks. The situation has created a better portfolio with a higher return in international exposure, given a lower risk. The point contains all risky investable assets and eliminates diversifiable risks by definition.

Furthermore, it is a high-risk point where the plans maximise the return regardless of the risk-taking. More than 80% of the recommended asset class is tilted towards international stocks. Regardless of risk, the local market would not offer an attractive return compared to global markets. However, a minimal allocation in fixed income is still required to keep the cash flow stream to support the liabilities requirement.

Figure 3.4 shows that KWAP asset allocation is outside the efficient frontier line. It means that KWAP has taken additional risks but reported a lower return. The three points have been derived from asset allocation last three years (2016–2018), as stated in Table 3.8. This recommendation is either for asset allocation increases or decreases derived based on the risk level taken by KWAP.

KWAP is on the right track since the allocation trend follows the global market's recommendation. KWAP has used the total return approach as its exclusive and main performance metric. The strategy offers a more reliable way to plan for retirement income, reducing some risks that are present in the investment portfolio and producing steady returns (KWAP, 2018).

SOA (2011) finds a significant rise in the funds and cash needed to fund the defined benefit system of the private sector. The decrease in high-quality corporate bond yields over the last few years led to

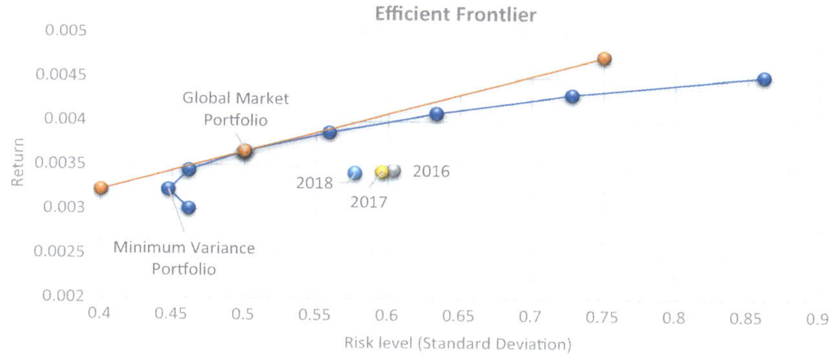

Fig. 3.4 Capital Market Line (CML) and efficient frontier graph with KWAP asset allocation (*Source* Authors' computation)

Table 3.8 KWAP's asset allocation for 2016–2018

Asset class/Year	*Asset allocation*			*Recommendation*
	2016 (%)	*2017 (%)*	*2018 (%)*	
Domestic equity	35.15	38.09	38.22	Decrease
Fixed income	47.69	44.17	40.90	Decrease
Money market	5.15	5.02	6.63	Increase
Real estate	1.46	1.70	2.12	Increase
International stocks	10.54	11.02	12.13	Increase

Source Authors' computation

the increase. However, contributions have increased due to the equities market's collapse and subsequently lost market returns.

Based on the latest three years of KWAP performance, KWAP focuses too much on traditional asset classes invested in equity and fixed income. The equity allocation between these two asset classes has increased while fixed income is decreasing. KWAP's fund feature has a long tenure where it can absorb any losses.

Based on the recommendation, KWAP should reduce fixed-income allocation and start having more international exposures or stocks. The money market seems surprisingly a safe asset allocation with the lowest risk exposure. However, it provides a steady return to the funds. Hence, increased allocation in the money market is the answer.

A study by Michas (2014) showed that investment has the potential for better performance in terms of returns and risk if Canadian pension funds diversify without restriction into international assets. It has also demonstrated that portfolio diversification in foreign securities can achieve substantial risk reduction advantages.

Pension Asset Allocation Consideration

The size of the portfolio affects allocation strategies. A small portfolio may lack the resources or qualifications to implement any complex strategy. However, KWAP is considered one of the significant pension funds and can implement complex strategies such as private equity and infrastructure. Extended tenure has increased pension funds' ability to invest in this asset.

KWAP should align the investment strategies with the ratio of average active participants to the average pensioner. Suppose there is a higher percentage of active participants. In that case, the plan can bear an additional risk since the plan has a longer tenure with more contributions than benefits. A higher proportion of retired lives (lower workforce age) pushes the funds to a higher liquidity requirement. Life Cycle Model has discussed this strategy, where young investors would afford to take a risk and allocate more financial capital to risky investments like equities.

SAA is not fixed but must continually be reviewed and updated as the client and longer-term market expectations change. Given the global outlook, pension providers must constantly check their strategic asset allocation by taking advantage of any chances that could increase the size of their fund without compromising their risk tolerance.

3.4 Conclusion

One of the main features of managing a pension fund is that the fund can pool investment risk across individuals and spread risk over a long tenure. KWAP, one of Malaysia's primary pension providers, has strategies for managing an optimal asset allocation to maximise the return.

Within 13 years, from 2007 to 2020, KWAP managed to have a positive ROI throughout these years. However, the results have shown that KWAP's performance has deteriorated since 2007. This trend is because the additional risk-taking by KWAP is not reflected by the additional alpha return as measured by the ROI.

A comprehensive risk management strategy is already in place to reduce potential negative consequences on its performance. KWAP has another big room to invest efficiently using Capital Market Line (CML) and Efficient Frontier as a baseline. The result shows that KWAP should reduce fixed-income allocation and have more international exposures or stocks. The money market seems surprisingly a safe asset allocation with the lowest risk exposure. However, it provides a steady return to the funds. Hence, increased allocation in the money market is the answer. The strategy will sustain KWAP to meet its future commitment.

References

Abu Bakar, N., & Rosbi, S. (2018). Efficient frontier analysis for portfolio investment in Malaysia stock market. *Science International, 30*(5), 723–729.

Abdul Rahman, M. I., & Lau, W.Y. (2023). Is the KWAP defined benefit pension fund sustainable in the long run? *International Journal of Banking and Finance, 18*(2), 97–126. https://doi.org/10.32890/ijbf2023.18.2.5

Alestalo, N., & Puttonen, V. (2006). Asset allocation in Finnish pension funds. *Journal of Pension Economics and Finance, 5*(1), 27–44. https://doi.org/10.1017/S1474747205002295

Anbalagan, V. (2022, January 31). Settle judges' pension claims out of court. *Free Malaysia Today*. https://www.freemalaysiatoday.com/category/nation/2022/01/31/settle-judges-pension-claims-out-of-court-say-lawyers/

Black, F. (1989). Should you use stocks to hedge your pension liability? *Financial Analysts Journal, 45*(1), 10–12.

Blake, David. (2001). UK pension fund management: How is asset allocation influenced by the valuation of liabilities? *The Pensions Institute, May*. https://doi.org/10.2139/ssrn.3610730

Blake, D., Lehmann, B. N., & Timmermann, A. (1999). Asset allocation dynamics and pension fund performance. *Journal of Business, 72*(4), 429–461. https://doi.org/10.1086/209623

Chernoff, J. (2003). Asset liability management back with a twist. *Pensions and Investments*.

Chun, G. H., Ciochetti, B. A., & Shilling, J. D. (2000). Pension-plan real estate investment in an asset-liability framework. In *Real estate economics* (Vol. 28, Issue 3, pp. 467–491). https://doi.org/10.1111/1540-6229.00809

Daim, N., & Yunus, A. (2021, September 28). Pension payments to reach RM46.6bil in 2030. *New Strait Times (NST)*. https://www.nst.com.my/news/nation/2021/09/731632/pm-pension-payments-reach-rm466bil-2030

FMT. (2022, February 21). government files appeal to restore legality of amended pension law. *Free Malaysia Today*. https://www.freemalaysiatoday.com/category/nation/2022/02/21/govt-wants-federal-court-to-restore-legality-of-amended-pension-law/

Hudson-Wilson, S., Gordon, J. N., Fabozzi, F. J., Anson, M. J. P., & Giliberto, S. M. (2005). Why real estate? *Journal of Portfolio Management, 20*(20), 12–22.

Irfan, M., & Lau, W.-Y. (2024). Asset allocation and performance of Malaysian civil service pension fund. *Australasian Accounting, Business and Finance Journal, 18*(1), 86–107. https://doi.org/10.14453/aabfj.v18i1.06

Ito, C. (1995). *Managing the risk of pension assets*. Risk Publications.

Jidwin, A. P., Ali, R., & Tuyon, J. (2012). The Malaysian employees provident fund's members' investment scheme: Survey of fund selection, performance and perceptions. *Management, 1*(9), 31–43.

KWAP. (2007). KWAP Annual Report 2007. *KWAP Website*. https://www.kwap.gov.my/EN/UsefulInformation/Publication/Annual%20Reports/KWAP%20Annual%20Report%202007.pdf

KWAP. (2017). KWAP Annual Report 2017. *KWAP Website*. https://www.kwap.gov.my/EN/UsefulInformation/Publication/Annual%20Reports/KWAP%20Annual%20Report%202017.pdf

KWAP. (2018). KWAP Annual Report 2018. *KWAP Website, 86*(3), 64–65. https://www.kwap.gov.my/EN/UsefulInformation/Publication/Annual%20Reports/KWAP%20Annual%20Report%202018.pdf

Leah, M., & Franco, M. (1997). Risk-adjusted performance. *Journal of Portfolio Management. Winter* 1997, *23*(2), 45–54.

Michas, N. A. (2014). Pension funds: More diversification. *Canadian Public Policy, 10*(1), 47–53.

OECD. (2020). Pension funds in figures 2020. *OECD, June*, pp. 1–5.

Papke, L. E. (1991). *The asset allocation of private pension plans.*

Parkaran, K. (2022, January 31). Court decision on pensions exposes a "Time Bomb." *Free Malaysia Today*. https://www.freemalaysiatoday.com/category/opinion/2022/01/31/court-decision-on-pensions-exposes-a-time-bomb/

SOA. (2011). The rising tide of pension contributions post-2008: How much and when? An analysis of funding for the U.S. private sector single-employer defined benefit system © 2011. *Society of Actuaries, February*.

Tunaru, R., Fabozzi, F., & Wu, T. (2006). Chinese equity market and the efficient frontier. *Applied Financial Economics Letters, 2*(2), 87–94. https://doi.org/10.1080/17446540500426755

CHAPTER 4

Can Future Pension Assets Meet Their Future Liabilities?

4.1 Background

The civil servant pension scheme is one of the benefits offered by the Malaysian government to public employees. Abd Manaf (2011) mentions that the service pension scheme was instituted in 1875 by the British administration. It is a non-contributory programme that provides financial assistance to retired government employees or surviving spouses. This pension scheme is a government-sponsored retirement plan with medical and pension payment benefits. The idea of a scheme is guaranteed for life adjusted slightly to address inflation or the cost of living.

The pension scheme is managed by a statutory body known as KWAP or Retirement Fund Incorporated, as the administrator and investment manager appointed by the Ministry of Finance (MOF) for pension fund collection and management since 2007 (KWAP, 2007). The Malaysian government pays the beneficiaries through KWAP as an agent. In addition to making the pension payment, the Malaysian government also adds more money to the KWAP to grow and use to cover future pension obligations.

The public pension in Malaysia recognises the value of offering survivor benefits, which are immediately important for the welfare of employees' families. This idea makes up for any loss of financial support for dependents, where the living partner and minor children are qualifying dependents. As a result, whether the deceased pensioner dies before or after

M. I. Abdul Rahman and W. Y. Lau, *Pension at Stake*,
https://doi.org/10.1007/978-981-97-2324-9_4

Table 4.1 Pension payment by Malaysian Government from 2001 to 2020

Component	*Pension payment*	*Gratuity payment*	*Total benefit paid*
Average Annual Growth Rate 2001–2020	7.60%	14.51%	8.03%

Source Economic Unit Report, Prime Minister's Department of Malaysia

retirement, the Malaysian government provides pension payments to their dependents.

In general, each retiree will receive two types of payment. The first is the monthly pension payment, and the second is the one-off gratuity payment upon retirement. Table 4.1 shows the average annual growth rate of 7.6% and 14.5% for pension and gratuity payments over the last 20 years. Table 4.1 shows an annual 8% increase in the Federal government's financial obligation over pension and gratuity.

Retirement Fund (Incorporated)

The Parliament of Malaysia enacted the Retirement Fund Act 2007 (Act 662) in March 2007 to establish a new statutory body named Retirement Fund (Incorporated). The act replaces the repealed Pensions Trust Fund Act 1991 (Act 454)—to assist the Federal government in funding its pension liability KWAP (2011). This retirement fund (Incorporated) is known as "Kumpulan Wang Persaraan (Diperbadankan)" (KWAP). It was launched with a capital start-up of RM500 million.

As Government-Linked Investment Companies (GLIC), KWAP is one of the three central bodies managing Malaysia's pension scheme besides EPF and LTAT. KWAP took over the Public Services Department (PSD) Post-Pension Services Division functions in 2015. It oversees pensions, gratuity, and other benefits granted under the merged fund (KWAP, 2017).

The Pensions Trust Fund's rights, obligations, activities, assets, and liabilities were transferred to KWAP by incorporation. The goal of KWAP is to oversee the fund created by Section 3 of the Retirement Fund Act of 2007 (Act 662). It seeks to maximise returns through benchmarking, a flexible investment framework, and prudent risk management. The fund will help finance the Federal government's pension obligation.

KWAP has full responsibility for investing and managing the respective fund. Any KWAP's new investments must follow policies set by the investment panel and approved by the board. These include a strategic asset allocation, which needs to be reviewed periodically to assure optimal returns from relatively low-risk investments.

The Investment Policy and Guidelines govern all KWAP's investing activities. However, the investment panel and the board will receive regular reports on the status and performance of KWAP's assets. As a sole fund manager for the government, assessing KWAP's performance and strategies is essential to ensure the government's financial sustainability in paying the pension and future obligations.

As shown in Table 4.2, the total fund size has increased from 2007 to 2018. The fund size reached RM141 billion in 2017 before declining slightly to RM137 billion in 2018. It is also noted that KWAP adhered wholly to adopting the Malaysian Financial Reporting Standards (MFRS) 9 in their financial accounts in 2018, which replaced the existing MFRS 139 (KWAP, 2018).

Nevertheless, despite the fund size of 137 billion in 2018, the gross and net Return on Investment (ROI) fell to 4.1% and 0.8%, the lowest recorded return in the past 12 years. This number raises whether KWAP can generate enough return from its assets to meet its future obligations. Hence, it is necessary to examine whether KWAP's future pension assets can cover its liabilities. Table 4.2 shows the KWAP's summary performance from 2007 to 2018.

Funding for Pension

Employers offer well-known retirement programmes: defined benefit (DB) and defined contribution (DC). The DB plan is the pension benefit in which the Malaysian government provides pension benefits to civil servants upon retirement based on final salary.

For the DB plan, the government, as the annuity provider, shall pay a specified annuity to the retirees. The benefit amounts are guaranteed no matter how underfunded the retiree's plan is. Regardless of ability or financial situation, the employer must pay the benefits.

Funding pension plans means putting aside financial assets dedicated to fulfilling the promised payments in the future. The amount of money that pension and annuity providers shall allocate each year is determined by how much expenses are allocated by actuaries each year. As a result,

Table 4.2 KWAP summary performance 2007–2018

Year 20XX	*2007*	*2008*	*2009*	*2010*	*2011*	*2012*	*2013*	*2014*	*2015*	*2016*	*2017*	*2018*
Fund size	48.08	52.04	61.5	70.52	78.93	88.73	99.92	109.43	118.37	125	140.8	136.51
Gross Invt Income	3.75	3.01	3.24	4.62	4.66	5.75	6.66	6.47	6.40	6.40	9.00	7.06
Net income	3.67	0.56	5.70	4.85	4.30	5.69	6.57	4.84	4.40	4.80	8.80	1.20
Gross ROI(%)	9.21%	5.86%	5.62%	7.07%	6.30%	6.84%	7.05%	6.15%	5.40%	5.40%	5.80%	4.10%
Net ROI(%)	9.79%	1.12%	10.04%	7.34%	5.75%	6.79%	6.97%	4.58%	3.26%	4.00%	7.00%	0.80%

Note Fund Size is measured in RM Billion, Gross Invt Income (Gross Investment Income) is measured in RM Billion, Net Income is measured in RM Billion, Gross Return on Investment (%), and Net Return on Investment (%)
Source KWAP Financial Report

building and sustaining a high level of assets to liabilities calls for fiscal restraint and extensive preparation.

Martell et al. (2013) demonstrate a reciprocal relationship between the public pension fund and states' finances. Thus, the funding situation of the government's DB-sponsored plans and other post-employment benefit programmes is closely tied to the government's financial stability.

The funding ratio is associated with three characteristics: the time a programme is started, the scope of the plan, and the generousness of benefits. When the plan has begun, older plans tend to have promised benefits over a more extended period without setting aside funds to fulfil the promises, which would lead to significant unfunded liability. Therefore, the predicted funded ratio will be smaller for the older plan.

Two funding issues have been raised: first, due to the stock market crash, the equity value held by the state and municipal plans is diminished, compromising their ability to remain funded. Second, many baby boomers are approaching retirement, and benefits for the retirees are expected to climb significantly (Munnell et al., 2011).

One of the main worries is how long the state and local plans can fulfil their commitments. In other words, will the budget for the plans run out? If so, when would it happen? Indeed, a retirement plan's assets-to-liabilities ratio illustrates how many years the plan can keep paying benefits in the event of no growth in the benefits plan, no extra contributions, and no returns on investments. Sponsors of the plan shall continue to contribute, notwithstanding the basic ratio, to reflect the changes over time. As the baby boomers retire, there is an expectation that the plan will generate returns on assets and the benefit payout will increase.

Performance of Managed Portfolios

The performance of managed portfolios across various asset classes was comprehensively examined by Blake et al. (1999). They also demonstrated the slow mean reversion in the funds' portfolio weights towards a time-varying strategic asset allocation. A data set on over 300 UK pension funds' asset holdings found that the ex-post returns from strategic asset allocation, market timing, and security selection show a relatively small cross-sectional variation.

Ryan and Fabozzi (2002) looked at the asset allocation of the typical pension fund and the liability structure to estimate the performance of defined benefit corporate pension plans in recent years. Funding levels and plan size are closely connected. Possible reasons for the pattern may be more sophisticated asset management and better discipline because not funding could significantly impact taxpayers in the future.

Winklevoss (2016) examines Monte Carlo simulations on asset return and inflation. It then generates a stochastic projection of a company's assets, liabilities, wages, and pension costs. Markets are so complex that one is virtually forced to use a computer simulation model to manage the likely impact of various policy alternatives. Regarding forecasting for KWAP's pension assets, Smirlock (1980) mentioned that private pension funds directly affect economic growth and stability, impacting the return to financial institutions. Private pension funds are the largest single category of personal savings in the United States. The savings function is related to economic growth because it makes capital formation possible. Since pension funds have a more significant impact on the financial market, much research indicates how to forecast the pension fund projection.

4.2 Methodology

Forecast Using Holt-Winter Model

This study uses secondary data from the KWAP financial report and Economic Unit Report, Prime Minister Department. This study computes the funded ratio from 2007 to 2018 since KWAP was established in 2007.

There are two types of benefits to the pensioner. There are pension payments and gratuity payments at the same time. Equation (4.1) illustrates the benefit paid as follows:

$$\text{Benefit paid} = \text{Pension Payment} + \text{Gratuity}. \tag{4.1}$$

The forecast seeks to determine the annual funding and expense needs. On the other hand, a pension prediction aims to determine the long-term financial effects of some anticipated or suggested adjustments.

Identifying Funded Status for 2021–2030

The idea is to determine the funded ratio by calculating the total asset market value and dividing it by the real retirement spending needs. If the

Table 4.3 Variables for the pension funded ratio

Item	*Details*	*Variables*	*Source*
A_t	Pension Assets	Represented by Gross Investment Return	KWAP Annual Report
L_L	Pension Obligations and Liabilities	Represented by Benefit Paid	KWAP

percentage is above 100%, then it indicate that the market value asset is sufficient to cover the pension in the future. Method 1 is presented by Equation (4.2) as below:

$$F(t) = \frac{A(t)}{L(t)}. \tag{4.2}$$

Using the funded ratio is the right way to analyse the ability of KWAP to decide whether KWAP has the right amount of assets to cover the liabilities. The funded ratio expresses the balance between available assets and liabilities in a pension fund's present financial situation. In other words, whether the pension fund has enough reserves to pay out pension benefits to existing and future members. A percentage is used to represent the funded ratio. However, due to the limited resources from this research, to examine KWAP's ability to pay liabilities, we have modified the formula as appears in Table 4.3:

Discounted the Underfunded For 2021–2030

To calculate these liabilities, the Governmental Accounting Standards Board (GASB) recommended discounting the stream of future benefits by a rate based on the estimated long-term yield of plan assets—roughly 3%. The majority of economists, however, agree that the discount rate should reflect the obligations' associated risk. Because most state laws guarantee benefits, a riskless rate is the appropriate discount factor, as stated in Equation (4.3) (Munnell et al., 2011):

$$PV of\, Pensions = \sum_{t=1}^{10} \frac{A(t) - L(t)}{(1+r)^t}, \tag{4.3}$$

where $A(t)$ denotes the Gross Investment Income, $L(t)$ represents the benefit paid at time t, and r is the discount rate.

The correct assumptions are critical to the forecast's usefulness since scenario assumptions influence crucial economic developments that could affect future pension costs. These assumptions must be consistent with the study's objectives, consider the plan's and sponsor's features, and reflect the plan's experience. One of the most crucial questions is, "What is a valuation assumption when it comes to scenario assumptions?"

Projection to Cover the Underfunded 2021–2030

Based on the amount we have discounted for ten years, we will predict the specific fund to be pumped into KWAP to cover the next ten years. This calculation is based on the average gross investment income from the fund size recorded since 2007. The idea is to measure how much funds the Malaysian government needs to inject into KWAP for investment purposes to generate income to cover future liabilities.

Understanding the forecast's goals will help one better grasp the sponsor's funding and expense expectations as well as their level of risk tolerance. At the same time, knowing the sponsor's expectations and risk tolerance will also help determine the study's scope, the scenario assumptions used, and the best way to present the forecast's findings (Sze, 1993).

Ignore the demographic assumption: project future employee populations. Such assumptions include the mortality, disability, termination and retirement patterns, and the number and distribution of new hires concerning sex, age, and pay. However, Sze (1993) stated that only small pension plans would be significantly affected by significant population and demographic changes in costs.

4.3 Results and Discussion

These numbers are forecasted based on the Holt-Winters Exponential Smoothing technique. The purpose of using Holt-Winters forecasting is to smooth a time series for F(t) and forecast. Exponential smoothing assigns exponentially decreasing weights and values against historical data to decrease the value of the weight for the older data.

Table 4.4 shows that KWAP is short of RM135 billion (nominal value) within the next ten years. In this case, the discount rate should reflect the risk associated with the liabilities. Hence, this computed data has used three situations: pessimistic, risk-free, and optimistic market outlooks. An optimistic market outlook offers a higher return than the other two scenarios.

Table 4.5 shows the present value of the funded gap between KWAP Gross Investment Income and Benefit Payout Liabilities by bar charts. It covers the highest discounted rate when the economy is doing well for the next ten years—using the 10-year cyclical recovery cycle. The optimistic situation covers about RM 100 billion, where the government can pass the pension obligation to KWAP.

The more distant the year, the more uncertain the projection is. Figures 4.1 and 4.2 show the funding gap between KWAP Gross Investment Income and Benefit Payout Liabilities.

The Public Service Department's responsibility for administering and processing pension benefits for government employees has been managed by KWAP following the Government Transformation Program. Retirees will benefit from this approach by receiving better service and timely pension payments. The Federal government has cut the contribution to KWAP since Accumulated Investment Income from KWAP performance is improving.

Table 4.4 Computed Funded Ratio from 2007 to 2020

Year	*Funded Ratio $F(t)$*	*$S(t) = A(t) - L(t)$ (RM Billion)*
2007	0.42	−4.81
2008	0.30	−7.00
2009	0.32	−6.97
2010	0.40	−6.90
2011	0.34	−8.85
2012	0.41	−8.22
2013	0.45	−8.13
2014	0.35	−11.76
2015	0.42	−8.74
2016	0.39	−10.20
2017	0.49	−9.43
2018	0.35	−13.17
2019*	0.41	−12.55
2020*	0.49	−9.52

*KWAP is yet to publish the 2019 and 2020 financial statements

Table 4.5 Computed Funded Ratio from 2021 to 2030

Year	*F(t)*	*S(t)* *(RM Billion)*	*Present Value (PV) of Cash Flow*		
			Pessimistic (1%)	*Risk-Free (3%)*	*Optimistic (5%)*
2021	0.43	−12.30	−12.18	−11.94	−11.71
2022	0.48	−11.68	−11.45	−11.01	−10.59
2023	0.47	−12.72	−12.34	−11.64	−10.98
2024	0.45	−13.89	−13.35	−12.34	−11.43
2025	0.49	−12.40	−11.80	−10.70	−9.72
2026	0.46	−14.20	−13.38	−11.89	−10.60
2027	0.50	−13.58	−12.66	−11.04	−9.65
2028	0.48	−14.62	−13.50	−11.54	−9.89
2029	0.47	−15.79	−14.44	−12.10	−10.18
2030	0.50	−14.30	−12.95	−10.64	−8.78
Total present value	–	−135.46	−128.03	−114.83	−103.52

Source Author's computation

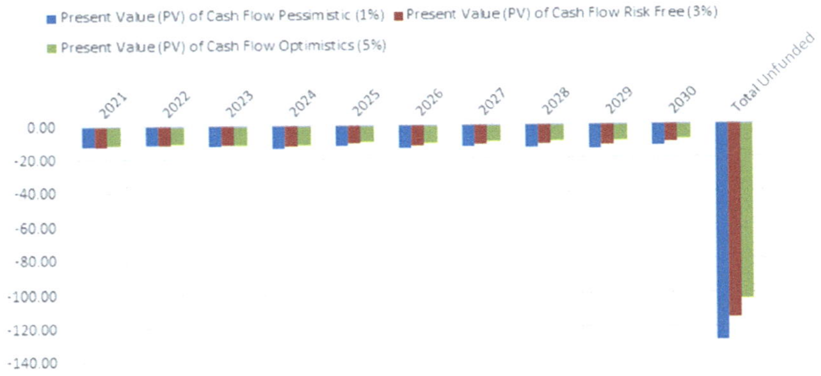

Fig. 4.1 Present value unfunded KWAP Pension Plan 2021–2030 (*Source* Author's computation)

Table 4.6 shows the additional funds that need to be injected into KWAP to cover the funding gap. This number is based on the average investment return for the past eleven years since KWAP was initiated. KWAP needs an additional RM135 billion for the fund's funding ratio

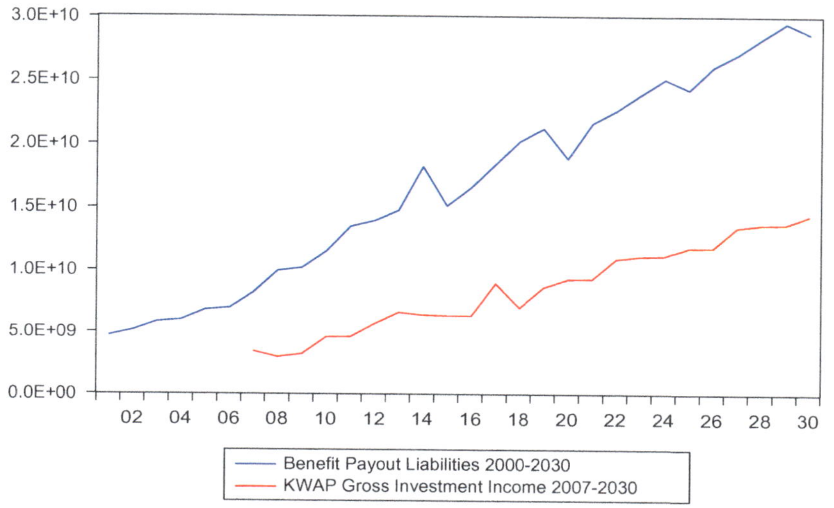

Fig. 4.2 KWAP investment income vs benefit payout liabilities for 2000–2030

generated by an additional RM2,174 billion. However, the optimistic market assumption will require a lower additional fund, RM1,662 billion, than a risk-free and pessimistic market outlook.

In most developing countries, rising old-age dependence ratios will put significant upward pressure on welfare spending over the next four decades. Many countries have begun a plan to reform their underfunded pension plans and improve benefit projections. In addition to enhancing

Table 4.6 Estimated additional fund required to cover unfunded plan for the next ten years

Year	*A(t) – L(t) (RM Billion)*	*Present Value (PV) of cash flow*		
		Pessimistic (1%) (RM Billion)	*Risk-Free (3%) (RM Billion)*	*Optimistic (5%) (RM Billion)*
Total Present Value	–135.46	–128.03	–114.83	–103.52
Additional Fund	–2,174.34	–2,055.06	–1,843.18	–1,661.70

Source Authors' computation

benefits, the government also studies cutting expenses to government spending on health and long-term care.

Still, some countries have made significant progress in ensuring the long-term viability of their welfare programmes. They have made substantial progress in securing the long-term sustainability of their pension schemes that protect welfare of the retirees. This is the importance of funding the pension scheme in ensuring its sustainability. KWAP's funded ratio needs to be increased to ensure the financial sustainability of the annual benefit paid out.

Plans cannot be fully funded overnight since building and maintaining substantial assets relative to liabilities takes years of discipline. Based on the asset, KWAP is an entity capable of paying future liabilities. However, asset liquidation is not an option that the government should not consider. KWAP must ensure the asset can generate sufficient investment income to pay the liabilities. Based on the forecasted number, the Malaysian government cannot hand over the mandate entirely to KWAP to manage pension liabilities in the next ten years.

Policy Recommendation

This study recommends a few measures so that the pension-funded ratio can be increased to more than 0.50 so that the government can eventually give a full mandate to KWAP in the long run.

Improve Investment Performance

Looking at the last published report by KWAP in 2018, the Gross Return on Investment (ROI) stands at 4.1%, with a fund size of RM137 billion undermanaged by KWAP. It is pertinent for the retirement fund to maintain a reasonable return parallel to the Capital Market expectation.

Release Timely Information

In addition, the timely publication of annual reports to the public is essential to ensure good governance of the state-sponsored pension scheme. There is a lag of 2 years before the financial report is made public on the website.

Increase Contribution

In the report, KWAP (2018) stated that "... the Federal Government contributes 5% of the total annual budgeted emolument of Federal Government employees while statutory bodies, local authorities, and agencies are required to contribute 17.5% of the basic salaries of pensionable employees monthly" to KWAP. In addition to pension contributions, the Federal government also contributed RM0.5 billion in funds to KWAP in 2018. In this respect, the relevant agencies can increase the contribution to KWAP to achieve economies of scale for the asset under management (AUM).

Restrict One Retiree's Entitlement to One Pension Benefit

It takes political courage to reduce the benefit of the existing/future retirees. It comes when the Malaysian government should implement stringent measures like restricting one retiree from receiving numerous pension benefits. A means test must be introduced to ensure a fair and equitable benefit. A pensioner should not be denied the subsistence benefit. However, pensioners should not be enriched by pension payments.

Include Longevity in the Analysis

The future pension-funded ratio is much riskier because of the uncertainty around survival probabilities. In this respect, defined benefit providers like KWAP must consider longevity risk in their pension benefit policy. The mortality risk's contribution to the overall risk of the future funded ratio becomes significantly less significant when market risk is considered (Hári et al., 2008). If the percentage of stock investments in the asset portfolio rises, the relative significance of longevity risk diminishes. The pension assets can only be developed with higher contributions from the Federal government and GLCs.

Increase the Mandate on a Staggered Basis

The future pension-funded ratio is much riskier because of the uncertainty around survival probabilities. In this respect, defined benefit providers like KWAP must consider longevity risk in their pension benefit policy. The mortality risk's contribution to the overall risk of the future funded ratio becomes significantly less significant when market risk is considered (Hári et al., 2008). If the percentage of stock investments in the asset portfolio rises, the relative significance of longevity risk diminishes. The pension assets can only be developed with higher contributions from the Federal government and GLCs.

Strengthen Corporate Governance

The incident of the RM4 billion loan from Retirement Fund Incorporated (KWAP) to SRC International Sdn Bhd shocked the financial markets. The loan was meant for a project by SRC's business plan to develop renewable energy. However, it was later found unsupported by any evidence, as revealed in the Court of Appeal hearing. It was further revealed that money was transferred to Switzerland when KWAP disbursed the loan in 2011 and 2012 (The Edge, 2021). This news raises the issue of corporate governance of state-sponsored pension funds.

4.4 Conclusion

The public sector delivers specific mandates or programmes to the general population and drives the country through growth and advancement. A future study on sustaining Malaysia's pension scheme is necessary as the fiscal budget to support the civil servant pension scheme has grown higher. The parliamentary debate has become a front-burner issue when the Ministry of Finance tables the national budget annually. This issue is worsened by the ever-increasing fiscal deficit the government has faced over the last twenty years.

This study examines Malaysia's statutory body, KWAP, which oversees the pension for civil servants. The conclusion emerges that, despite not having a full federal mandate yet to cover pension liabilities, in the aggregate, KWAP is making solid progress towards funding by growing pension assets from RM500 million as fund capital into a fund worth RM137 billion. However, a snapshot of assets and liabilities is insufficient to assess the long-term viability of KWAP's goals. Therefore, this study examines how successful programmes provide yearly paid benefits.

The underlying premise is that the KWAP is a state where that needs more funding from the Malaysian government. Based on the seven recommendations above, the government must balance the civil service pension system's viability and benefits. Given the increased life expectancy and ageing society Malaysia will eventually face in 2030, a new legal framework, such as restricting individual retirees from having more than one pension benefit, must be instituted before it is too late.

References

Abd Manaf, N. H. (2011). Public administration in Southeast Asia. *Taylor and Francis Group, 309–309*,. https://doi.org/10.4135/9781452283241.n50

Blake, David, Lehmann, B. N., & Timmermann, A. (1999). Asset Allocation Dynamics and Pension Fund Performance. *Journal of Business*, *72*(4), 429–461. https://doi.org/10.1086/209623

Hári, N., De Waegenaere, A., Melenberg, B., & Nijman, T. E. (2008). Longevity risk in portfolios of pension annuities. *Insurance: Mathematics and Economics*, *42*(2), 505–519. https://doi.org/10.1016/j.insmatheco.2007.01.012

Irfan, M., & Lau, W.-Y. (2024). Asset allocation and performance of Malaysian civil service pension fund. *Australasian Accounting, Business and Finance Journal*, *18*(1), 86–107. https://doi.org/10.14453/aabfj.v18i1.06

KWAP. (2007). KWAP Annual Report 2007. *KWAP Website*. https://www.kwap.gov.my/EN/UsefulInformation/Publication/Annual Reports/KWAP Annual Report 2007.pdf

KWAP. (2011). KWAP Annual Report 2011. *Kumpulan Wang Persaraan (Diperbadankan)*, *82*(10), 4.

KWAP. (2017). KWAP Annual Report 2017. *KWAP Website*. https://www.kwap.gov.my/EN/UsefulInformation/Publication/Annual Reports/KWAP Annual Report 2017.pdf

KWAP. (2018). KWAP Annual Report 2018. *KWAP Website*, *86*(3), 64–65. https://www.kwap.gov.my/EN/UsefulInformation/Publication/Annual Reports/KWAP Annual Report 2018.pdf

Martell, C. R., Kioko, S. N., & Moldogaziev, T. (2013). Impact of unfunded pension obligations on credit quality of state governments. *Public Budgeting and Finance*, *33*(3), 24–54. https://doi.org/10.1111/j.1540-5850.2013.12013.x

Munnell, A. H., Aubry, J. P., & Quinby, L. (2011). Public pension funding in practice. *Journal of Pension Economics and Finance*, *10*(2), 247–268. https://doi.org/10.1017/S1474747211000126

Ryan, R. J., & Fabozzi, F. J. (2002). Rethinking pension liabilities and asset allocation. *Journal of Portfolio Management*, *28*(4), 7-15+3. https://doi.org/10.3905/jpm.2002.319849

Smirlock, M. (1980). Private Pension Fund Assets: Projected Growth to 1990. *The Journal of Risk and Insurance*, *47*(2), 321. https://doi.org/10.2307/252335

Sze, M. (1993). The process of pension forecasting. *Journal of Actuarial Practice 1993–2006*. 160. http://digitalcommons.unl.edu/joap/160 retrieved from https://core.ac.uk/download/pdf/127444889.pdf.

Winklevoss, H. E. (2016). Plasm: Pension Liability and Asset Simulation Model. *The Journal of Finance*, *37*(2).

CHAPTER 5

Is the Defined Benefit Pension Fund Sustainable in the Long Run?

5.1 Defined Benefit Plan and Its Sustainability

In the Defined Benefit (DB) plan, the annuity provider must pay a specified annuity to the retirees. Benefit amounts are guaranteed regardless of whether the retiree's DB plan is underfunded. In other words, the benefit to be paid becomes the employer's obligation, irrespective of its financial condition or capacity.

Hence, the financial sustainability of the DB plan scheme refers to the annuity provider's capacity to fulfil the short-term and long-term commitments in paying pensions. The short-term commitment refers to the ability to finance the current debt to pay current pensioners by considering the current assets and liabilities. Long-term obligations, also known as implicit debt, refer to the ability to finance future pension that considers future expenditures and revenues (Barr & Diamond, 2009; Holzmann et al., 2004).

Despite the rising pension costs, the Federal Constitution of Malaysia safeguards the pension system. It guarantees solvency (the assets must equal liabilities) (Lee, 1997). When the pension deficit becomes too large and persists, the pension scheme becomes unsustainable, requiring the reviewing and changing of pension parameters to ensure sustainability. Hence, Barr and Diamond (2009) argue that any pension expenditure shall be compatible with one country's ability to finance retirees'

M. I. Abdul Rahman and W. Y. Lau, *Pension at Stake*,
https://doi.org/10.1007/978-981-97-2324-9_5

consumption, investment return from the pension assets, and the fund manager's ability to raise revenues.

The revenues must be sufficient to cover the liabilities and to ensure financial sustainability in the long run. The ability to finance future expenditures will depend on the fund contribution, the interest earned on the assets, and the pension promises to the current and future retirees (Barr & Diamond, 2006). A pension deficit means the contribution collection and returns do not match the payments to pensions.

When a pension deficit occurs, the pension scheme becomes financially unsustainable. It thus, creates a pension debt that the government needs to finance through its revenue or by raising taxes. Some governments have responded to underfunded pensions with a wave of pension reforms that seek to limit benefits for current employees and alter the benefit structure for future employees.

Malaysia's long-term sustainability pension relies on the KWAP pension fund's ability to generate a return in paying out pensions to present and future retirees. Nevertheless, without employee contribution, the government would encounter problems accumulating financial reserves for investing and getting the required returns for ongoing payments (Lee, 1997).

Since the KWAP has operated for more than 12 years, the total fund size has gradually increased. In 2007, the total fund was recorded at RM47.42 billion, the highest, amounting to RM141 billion in 2017 before declining to RM137 billion in 2018. In 2018, the Malaysian Financial Reporting Standards (MFRS) 9 was fully adopted, replacing the existing MFRS 139 (KWAP, 2018).

In general, each retiree will receive two types of payment. The first is the monthly pension payment, and the second is the one-off gratuity upon retirement. Table 5.1 shows the annual growth rate of 7.6% and 14.5% for pension and gratuity payments over the last 20 years. Table 5.1 also shows an annual 8% increase in the Federal government's financial obligation to pension and gratuity payments.

Besides the government pension scheme, two other prominent pension schemes in Malaysia are the Employee Provident Fund (EPF) and the Armed Forces Fund Board (LTAT). The EPF manages a defined pension scheme contribution for private sector employees. At the same time, the LTAT oversees compulsory and voluntary pension contributions for non-pensionable and pensionable armed forces specific to industries. However, this study does not discuss these pension schemes under the EPF and

Table 5.1 Pension payment by the Malaysian government from 2001 to 2020

Component	*Pension payment (%)*	*Gratuity payment (%)*	*Total benefit paid (%)*
Average annual growth rate 2001–2020	7.60	14.51%	8.03%

Note Sourced from the Economic Unit Report 2001–2020, Prime Minister's Department

LTAT. The private retirement scheme and the basic state scheme are also not discussed.

Currently, the public employee pension is funded by the State and Federal governments' annual contribution to the KWAP.[1] There is an ongoing issue that the pension cost has increased over many years. The retirement cost in the 2019 Federal Budget stood at 27.06 billion of the operating expenditure (OPEX).[2] What is the ideal contribution rate from the government agency, the KWAP? In addition, what is the required return from the investment undertaken by the Federal government to ensure the sustainability of the pension fund in the long term? These questions remain unaddressed in the literature.

This next part of the chapter is organised as follows. Section 2 highlights the relevant literature, followed by the data collection and methodology in Sect. 3. Section 4 discusses the results, while the last section concludes this study.

Investment Policy

The nature of pension funds is to decide on the best investment policy and implement those policies. Any risk taken is a cost to the fund management. Ambachtsheer (1994) has explained two implementation choices. One is to take the lowest-risk-cost path with due diligence and prudence. In contrast, another takes the additional bundle of risks and costs, expecting the economic payoff (additional fund return) to justify the additional cost and risk assumed. As such, pension fund management involves creating one of these two relationships conceptually over time as follows:

$$\boldsymbol{Policy\ Return} = \boldsymbol{f(Policy\ RiskCost)} \text{ or}$$

$$\textit{\textbf{Policy Return}} + \textit{\textbf{Additional Return}} = f(\textit{\textbf{Policy RiskCost}}, \textit{\textbf{Additional Risk}})$$

The idea of investment choices is to maximise return. However, a pension fund cannot just maximise its returns using the traditional method. Chernoff (2003) has explained that one way to manage a pension fund is by matching pension assets against pension liabilities. Besides providing pension liabilities to the pensioners, Rudolf and Ziemba (2004) have argued that pension fund sponsors have the secondary goal of achieving an "earning spread" to reduce future liabilities.

For example, the Malaysia pension funds have been studied by Jidwin et al. (2012) regarding their fund selection, performance, and perception survey. The results revealed that members' experiences of investment performances and risk-taking were mixed. It is challenging for pension fund managers to fulfil a guaranteed minimum return to the contributors as they have to consider the performance return and risk perception aspects.

Funding Pension

Two prominent employer-sponsored retirement plans: defined benefit (DB) and defined contribution (DC). The DB plan is the pension benefit in which the Malaysian government guarantees pension benefits to the employee upon retirement based on the employee's final salary scale. Hence, the Malaysian government faces an increasing financial burden regarding pensions and gratuities payable. The government is responsible for the pension obligations of civil officials' pensions and gratuities. According to economic reports, Malaysia's expenditure on pensions and gratuities has risen yearly (MOF, 2019). According to Barr and Diamond (2009), any pension expenditure must align with the nation's capacity to pay for retirees' consumption, the investment returns from the pension assets, and the fund manager's capacity to generate income in the future.

For the DB plan, the government, as the annuity provider, must pay a specified annuity to the retirees. The benefits are guaranteed regardless of whether the retiree's plan is underfunded. The benefit amounts are the employer's obligation, irrespective of its financial condition or capacity.

Funding pension plans means putting aside financial assets dedicated to fulfilling the promised payments in the future. The amount of money that pension and annuity providers should allocate each year is determined by how much expenses are allocated by actuaries each year. Hence, establishing and maintaining a high level of assets relative to liabilities requires fiscal discipline and many years of planning.

Martell et al. (2013) demonstrate a reciprocal relationship between the public pension fund and states' finances. Thus, any government's financial health is inextricably linked to the funding status of its DB-sponsored plans and other post-employment benefit programmes.

The funding ratio is associated with the plan's three characteristics: the time the programme is commenced, plan size, and the generosity of benefits. When the plan has started, older plans tend to have promised benefits over a more extended period without setting aside funds to fulfil the promises, which would lead to significant unfunded liability. Therefore, the older the plan, the lower the expected funded ratio.

Two funding issues have been raised: First, the stock market's collapse reduces the equity value held by the state and local plans, thus undermining the funded status of all stated and local plans. Second, many baby boomers are about to retire, which means that benefits are slated to increase sharply (Munnell et al., 2011).

One of the key concerns is how long the state and local plans can keep up with their promises. In other words, are the plans going to run out of cash? If so, when would it happen? Indeed, a retirement plan's assets-to-liabilities ratio illustrates how many years the plan can keep paying benefits in the event of no other investment returns, no additional contribution, and no growth in the scheme benefits. Sponsors of the plan shall continue to contribute, notwithstanding the basic ratio, to reflect the changes over time. As the baby boomers retire, there is an expectation that the plan will generate returns on assets and that the benefit payout will increase.

Asset Allocation

An asset class is a group of assets with similar investment characteristics and subject to the same regulations. Each asset class shall carry risk factors such as equity market risk, interest rates, inflation, or currency risk. Thus, portfolio weighting for an asset class helps manage the portfolio's risk exposure. Asset allocation influences the return to the retirement fund.

An optimal asset allocation is when the pension plan sponsor dynamically weighs the portfolio. Strategic Asset Allocation (SAA) is the highest decision-making level in the investment process. Hence, Alestalo and

Puttonen (2006) have discussed pension fund portfolio management in two steps.

The first is when the sponsoring company identifies steps to invest in broad asset classes, known as strategic asset allocation, which heavily affects a pension fund's performance. The asset classes include, but are not limited to, fixed income, equity, money market instruments, real estate, private equity, or even commodities.

The second is asset allocation implementation via internal or external fund managers. The role of fund managers is critical in selecting the right investment strategies or security processes. The sponsor shall consider the fund manager with a higher information ratio, indicating additional spread or alpha over additional unit risk.

The literature has highlighted two extreme views on optimal asset allocation. From one perspective, bonds are the sole option to align assets with liabilities. At the same time, another view advises that the assets should have equity exposure. The potential asset classes include fixed income, equity, money market, and alternative investments such as real estate, private equity, and commodities. Traditionally, equity and fixed income are the main asset classes for pension funds, whereas alternative investments are growing in demand.

For example, the OECD (2020) report shows that OECD pension funds are primarily invested in equities and fixed-income asset classes. A total of 16 of the 36 OECD countries have more than 75% of their pension portfolios in equities and bonds. However, Papke (1991) found that the asset allocation of the US private pension funds in terms of fixed income and equities depends on the type of employers. Single-employer plans tend to have about 60% fixed-income and 20% equity securities. The smaller single employers invest 50% and 20% in fixed-income and equity securities. They found that the equity allocation increased its share from 48% in 1991 to 57% in 2001. Blake et al. (1999) found that 300 UK pension funds have a higher equity allocation than fixed-income securities. However, this study concentrates on pension performance rather than asset allocation.

5.2 Methodology

This study has adopted a few assumptions from the Malaysian Public Service Department Post-Service Division to project the retirement fund. The goal is to produce a retirement fund cash flow for pensioners of

Malaysia's civil service under a few scenarios. The objective is to estimate the required return needed to sustain the retirement fund for Malaysia's civil servants.

Monthly Pension Payment

First, one needs to understand the type of pension benefits the Malaysian government offers. The civil servant who is eligible for a pension in Malaysia is the one who retires or is asked to retire from government service, and s/he is eligible for the pension benefits (JPA, 2021). For a typically defined benefit pension plan, the Malaysian government pledges a monthly pension payment according to the employee's final salary and years of service using a specific formula as follows:

$$\textbf{\textit{Pension Payment (Monthly)}} = \frac{1}{600} \times \textbf{\textit{Last Drawn Salary}} \times \textbf{\textit{Service Months}}$$

The formula, however, is limited to a pension of three-fifths of the last basic salary (after 30 years or 360 months of the recognised service period). In other words, the maximum number of months recognised is limited to 360 months (30 years of service). A pensionable officer who has worked for over 30 years is not eligible for additional months of service in the pension calculation.

Service Gratuity Payment

The formula is as follows:

$$\textbf{\textit{Gratuity Payment}} = \textbf{\textit{Last Drawn Salary}} \times \textbf{\textit{months of reckonable service}} \times 7.5\%$$

This one lump sum payment by the Malaysian government to the retirees is in appreciation for their services to the government.

Cash Award in Place of Leaves

The Malaysian government provides for the Cash Award in place of Leave (GCR) for public service officers. The GCR is an official recognition of unused leave due to service necessity. It is accumulated following the terms under the pension regulations. This benefit is known as a "Golden

Handshake" for Malaysian civil servants. The provision for Cash Award in place of the Accumulated Leave was enacted on 1 January 1974 under Service Circular No. 1/1974 and is granted to public service personnel who will retire on or after 1 January 1974 (JPA, 2021). The formula is as follows:

$$\boldsymbol{Cash\ Award} = \frac{1}{30} \times (\boldsymbol{Last\ Drawn\ Salary} + \boldsymbol{Fixed\ Allowances}) \times \boldsymbol{Number\ of\ Leave}$$

As of August 2020, the maximum number of claimable days is up to 180 days. However, the Malaysian government can scrutinise and amend any mistakes in the officer leave record when approving the claim.

Scenario Analysis

Scenario analysis is one of the methods to assess portfolio value changes in response to certain conditions. The idea is to study how unfortunate events and worst-case scenarios (tail risk) influence the portfolio value. Hence, scenario analysis is proposed using the pension formula to find the required return for the civil service pension fund under a few scenarios and assumptions.

This study estimates the average investment return throughout the defined benefits period to cover future obligations under various scenarios. Figure 5.1 shows how the required returns are generated using different assumptions and constraints. This study has made assumptions about the input of the variables. Table 5.2 summarises the input range for four variables in generating the scenario-based analysis.

The rationale for the scenario-based assumptions is as follows:

i. Inflation Assumption
The inflation assumption is that every pensioner is eligible for the 2% monthly annuity increment for each year (JPA, 2021)

ii. Salary Increment
The Malaysian government has provided a salary increment of 3% each year starting from 2013 (JPA, 2021).

iii. Mortality Rate
This study ignores the table of mortality probability that projects how long civil servants will live after retirement. Life expectancy

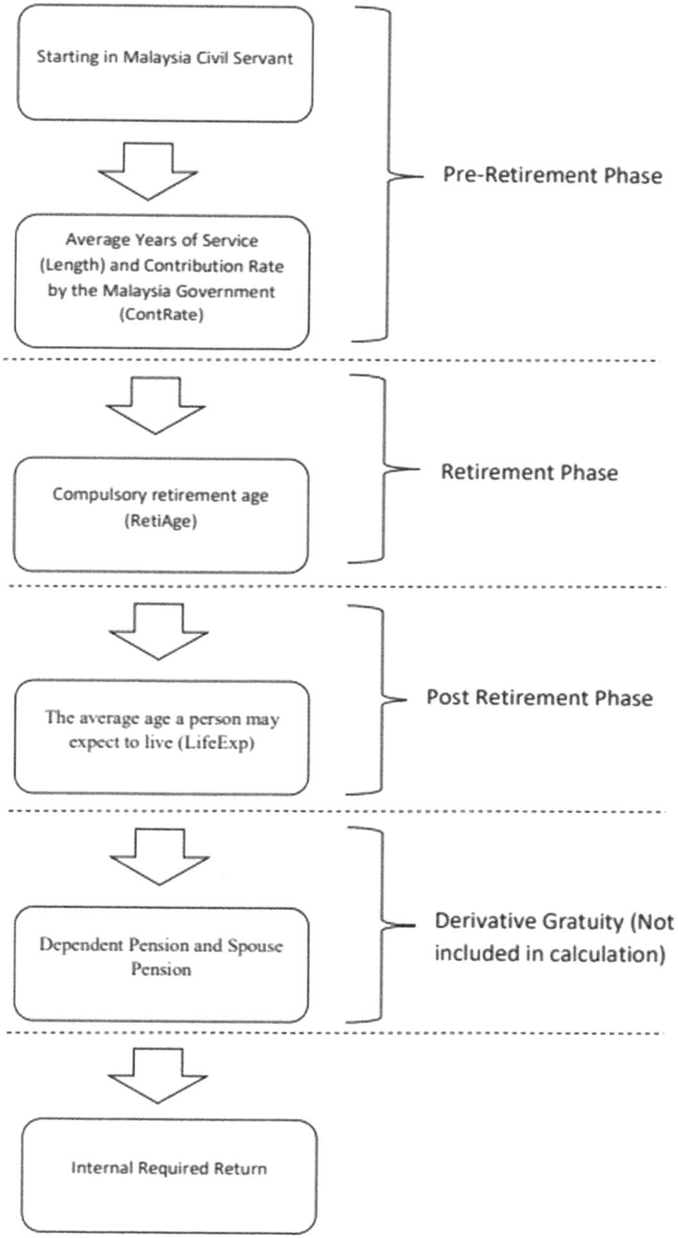

Fig. 5.1 Workflow of the scenario analysis (*Note* Based on the Authors' sketch)

Table 5.2 Input range for the variables used in the required return simulation

Variable	*Unit*	*Description*	*Range*
Contribution Rate (ContRate)	Percentage	Defined benefit contribution by the Malaysian government based on salary per month	3–15%
Average year of service (Length)	Years	Length of service in government sector	10, 20, 30, and 40 years
Retirement Age (RetiAge)	Years	Compulsory retirement age	55, 56,58, and 60 years old
Life Expectancy (LifeExp)	Years	The average period a person may expect to live	75, 80, 85, 90, and 95 years old

shall be considered one of the possibilities when calculating future liabilities.

iv. Optional Retirement Age
Malaysia's pension scheme offers an optional retirement age for those who have fulfilled the criteria. A civil servant with a pension who has reached the age of 40 and has a recognised period of service of no less than ten years may apply for optional retirement, whereby the application must go through the Head of the Department where the member serves. However, this study may ignore the matter of optional retirement in the calculation.

v. Leave Claim
This study assumes that civil servants can claim a maximum leave of 180 days.

vi. Dependent Pension and Spouse Pension
The pension scheme in Malaysia also extends pension benefits to the deceased officer's dependants who passed away while still in the service or upon retirement. The extension benefit is known as a derivative gratuity or derivative pension. However, this study may ignore the matter of derivative gratuity in the retirement fund calculation.

Internal Rate of Return

This study defines the required return via the internal rate of return (IRR). The IRR is a financial analysis metric to estimate a potential investment's profitability. In a discounted cash flow analysis, the IRR is a discount rate that equals all cash flows' net present value (NPV) to zero. The IRR relies on the same formula as the NPV does. One has to remember that the IRR is not the actual dollar value of the project. It is the annual return that makes the NPV equal to zero. The IRR is calculated using the same concept as the NPV, except it sets the NPV as equal to zero. The IRR is ideal for capital budgeting analysis and for understanding and comparing the potential annual rate of return over time, as in Eq. 5.1 below:

$$NPV = \sum_{t=1}^{T} \frac{C_t}{(1 + IRR)^t}. \tag{5.1}$$

To find the right amount of return and liabilities, the NPV must be equal to zero. Equation 5.2 is stated as below:

$$0 = \sum_{t=1}^{T} \frac{C_t}{(1 + IRR)^t}. \tag{5.2}$$

where C_t denotes the cash flow at that time, t.

The IRR indicates the annualised rate of return for a given investment, no matter how far into the future, and the projected future cash flow. In this study, the IRR is the annual growth rate that an investment is likely to generate to ensure the fund can pay the liabilities in the future.

Regression

Besides the scenario analysis, this study attempts to model and investigate the factors influencing the retirement fund required to return in Malaysia using the ordinary least square (OLS) over 560 scenarios. A scenario simulation is designed to examine the retirement plan rate of return to fund sufficient pension liabilities in the future.

This study intends to determine the rate of return the Malaysian government should maintain to sustain the pension fund in the long run.

Accordingly, the formula used is as follows:

$$\textbf{\textit{RequiredReturn(IRR)}} = \textbf{\textit{f(ContRate, LifeExp, Length, RetiAge)}}$$

where

> ContRate denotes the contribution rate when the Malaysian government puts aside a fund for the retirement fund;
> LifeExp represents life expectancy for the post-retirement period;
> Length means the years of service of a civil servant; and
> RetiAge indicates the retirement age.

Hypothesis:

As pointed out earlier, this study aims to investigate the impact of the independent variables on the required rate of return of the Malaysian pension fund investment. Overall, the contribution rate, length of service, and retirement age shall negatively affect the required rate of return needed by the fund. However, a higher life expectancy shall lead to a higher required rate of return. The hypotheses of this study are as follows:

- H_1: Contribution Rate is negatively associated with the required rate of return.
- H_2: Life Expectancy is positively associated with the required rate of return.
- H_3: Length of Service is negatively associated with the required rate of return.
- H_4: Retirement Age is negatively associated with the required rate of return.

When the contribution rate, length of service, and retirement age increase, the required return generated from the KWAP pension fund will be lower. Hence, these three variables are expected to be negatively associated with the required rate of return (H_1, H_3, and H_4). On the other hand, the longer the retiree's life expectancy, the required rate of return generated by the KWAP pension fund will be higher (H_2).

5.3 Results

Scenario Analysis Findings

The findings of the ***Required Rate of Return*** are summarised in Table 5.3, indicating the descriptive statistics based on the simulation of the 560 scenarios. The simulation shows the required rate of return that the Malaysian pension fund needs to achieve based on the parameters set up in this study.

The maximum required return is 69.28% of the investment return for the 560 scenarios. The policy required the highest required return when the contribution rate was 3%, and the length of services was ten years, regardless of the retirement age and life expectancy. However, it is possible to generate as low as 13.75% of the required return to ensure the sustainability of the retirement plan. This level can be achieved by a contribution rate of 15% and at least 40 years in public service.

Out of the 560 scenarios, the mean of the required return was 29.67%, with a standard error of 0.65%. Based on the kurtosis and skewness, the actual return distribution was not expected since the mean, median, and mode values differed. This distribution has skewed to the left as the mode exceeded the median and mean. Tables 5.4, 5.5, 5.6, and 5.7 show the 560 scenarios that used different investment returns.

Table 5.3 Descriptive statistics of simulation-based on 560 scenarios

Required return	
Mean	0.2967
Standard error	0.0065
Median	0.2437
Mode	0.5146
Standard deviation	0.1536
Sample variance	0.0236
Kurtosis	0.0158
Skewness	1.0825
Range	0.5562
Minimum	0.1365
Maximum	0.6928
Sum	166.15
Count	560

Table 5.4 Required rate of return at the retirement age of 55 years

Length of services (Years)	*Life expectancy (years)*	*Contribution rate*						
		3%	*5%*	*7%*	*9%*	*10%*	*13%*	*15%*
10	75	69.2781%	60.7906%	55.3933%	51.4602%	49.8361%	45.8557%	43.7234%
	80	69.2782%	60.7909%	55.3940%	51.4614%	49.8376%	45.8583%	43.7269%
	85	69.2782%	60.7910%	55.3941%	51.4615%	49.8378%	45.8587%	43.7275%
	90	69.2782%	60.7910%	55.3941%	51.4615%	48.6328%	45.8588%	43.7277%
	95	69.2782%	60.7910%	54.7119%	51.4616%	49.8378%	45.7418%	43.7277%
20	75	35.0688%	31.5430%	29.2600%	27.5747%	26.8732%	25.1392%	24.2010%
	80	35.0760%	31.5552%	29.2773%	27.5972%	26.8982%	25.1719%	24.2388%
	85	35.0778%	31.5586%	29.2826%	27.6045%	26.9066%	25.1835%	24.2528%
	90	35.0782%	31.5596%	29.2842%	27.6068%	26.9094%	25.1877%	24.2579%
	95	35.0783%	31.5599%	29.2847%	27.6076%	26.9103%	25.1891%	24.2599%
30	75	24.5514%	22.3557%	20.9222%	19.8574%	19.4124%	18.3075%	17.7067%
	80	24.5761%	22.3906%	20.9658%	19.9089%	19.4676%	18.3731%	17.7788%
	85	24.5852%	22.4044%	20.9840%	19.9313%	19.4920%	18.4034%	17.8128%
	90	24.5885%	22.4099%	20.9917%	19.9412%	19.5030%	18.4176%	17.8291%
	95	24.5897%	22.4121%	20.9950%	19.9455%	19.5079%	18.4242%	17.8369%
40	75	18.8884%	17.2773%	16.2190%	15.4293%	15.0983%	14.2738%	13.8239%
	80	18.9287%	17.3294%	16.2808%	15.4996%	15.1724%	14.3585%	13.9149%
	85	18.9470%	17.3547%	16.3120%	15.5360%	15.2113%	14.4043%	13.9649%
	90	18.9554%	17.3670%	16.3278%	15.5551%	15.2320%	14.4294%	13.9928%
	95	18.9592%	17.3731%	16.3360%	15.5652%	15.2430%	14.4433%	14.0085%

Table 5.5 Required rate of return at the retirement age of 56 years

Length of services (Years)	*Life expectancy (Years)*	*Contribution rate*						
		3%	*5%*	*7%*	*9%*	*10%*	*13%*	*15%*
10	75	69.2780%	60.7904%	55.3929%	51.4595%	49.8353%	45.8543%	43.7216%
	80	69.2782%	60.7909%	55.3940%	51.4613%	49.8375%	45.8581%	43.7266%
	85	69.2782%	60.7903%	55.3941%	51.4615%	49.8378%	45.8587%	43.7275%
	90	69.2782%	60.7910%	55.3941%	51.4615%	48.6328%	45.8588%	43.7277%
	95	69.2782%	60.7910%	55.3941%	51.4616%	49.8378%	45.8567%	43.7277%
20	75	35.0656%	31.5380%	29.2532%	27.5663%	26.8640%	25.1275%	24.1877%
	80	35.0752%	31.5538%	29.2753%	27.5945%	26.8952%	25.1677%	24.2340%
	85	35.0776%	31.5583%	29.2820%	27.6036%	26.9055%	25.1820%	24.2510%
	90	35.0781%	31.5595%	29.2840%	27.6065%	26.9090%	25.1871%	24.2573%
	95	35.0783%	31.5598%	29.2846%	27.6075%	26.9102%	25.1890%	24.2596%
30	75	24.5426%	22.3439%	20.9078%	19.8408%	19.3947%	18.2870%	17.6844%
	80	24.5730%	22.3859%	20.9598%	19.9017%	19.4598%	18.3637%	17.7683%
	85	24.5840%	22.4025%	20.9815%	19.9282%	19.4886%	18.3990%	17.8078%
	90	24.5880%	22.4091%	20.9907%	19.9398%	19.5014%	18.4155%	17.8267%
	95	24.5895%	22.4118%	20.9945%	19.9449%	19.5072%	18.4233%	17.8358%
40	75	18.8758%	17.2614%	16.2006%	15.4087%	15.0767%	14.2495%	13.7979%
	80	18.9229%	17.3218%	16.2716%	15.4890%	15.1612%	14.3455%	13.9009%
	85	18.9443%	17.3510%	16.3073%	15.5304%	15.2054%	14.3972%	13.9571%
	90	18.9542%	17.3652%	16.3254%	15.5522%	15.2288%	14.4255%	13.9885%
	95	18.9587%	17.3722%	16.3347%	15.5637%	15.2413%	14.4411%	14.0061%

Table 5.6 Required rate of return at the retirement age of 58 years

Length of services	*Life expectancy (years)*	*Contribution rate*						
(Years)		*3%*	*5%*	*7%*	*9%*	*10%*	*13%*	*15%*
10	75	69.2780%	60.7904%	55.3929%	51.4595%	49.8353%	45.8543%	43.7216%
	80	69.2782%	60.7909%	55.3940%	51.4613%	49.8375%	45.8581%	43.7266%
	85	69.2782%	60.7903%	55.3941%	51.4615%	49.8378%	45.8587%	43.7275%
	90	69.2782%	60.7910%	55.3941%	51.4615%	48.6328%	45.8588%	43.7277%
	95	69.2782%	60.7910%	55.3941%	51.4616%	49.8378%	45.8567%	43.7277%
20	75	35.0561%	31.5234%	29.2339%	27.5424%	26.8379%	25.0952%	24.1515%
	80	35.0729%	31.5498%	29.2694%	27.5868%	26.8866%	25.1564%	24.2208%
	85	35.0770%	31.5571%	29.2802%	27.6011%	26.9027%	25.1780%	24.2461%
	90	35.0780%	31.5592%	29.2835%	27.6057%	26.9081%	25.1857%	24.2555%
	95	35.0782%	31.5597%	29.2845%	27.6072%	26.9098%	25.1884%	24.2589%
30	75	24.5187%	22.3125%	20.8702%	19.7978%	19.3492%	18.2347%	17.6280%
	80	24.5643%	22.3736%	20.9442%	19.8832%	19.4399%	18.3400%	17.7422%
	85	24.5808%	22.3976%	20.9750%	19.9201%	19.4797%	18.3880%	17.7954%
	90	24.5869%	22.4072%	20.9879%	19.9362%	19.4975%	18.4104%	17.8208%
	95	24.5891%	22.4110%	20.9934%	19.9434%	19.5054%	18.4209%	17.8329%
40	75	18.8434%	17.2216%	16.1547%	15.3578%	15.0236%	14.1903%	13.7350%
	80	18.9084%	17.3028%	16.2490%	15.4631%	15.1339%	14.3142%	13.8670%
	85	18.9377%	17.3417%	16.2959%	15.5170%	15.1910%	14.3802%	13.9385%
	90	18.9511%	17.3607%	16.3196%	15.5451%	15.2211%	14.4161%	13.9781%
	95	18.9573%	17.3699%	16.3317%	15.5599%	15.2372%	14.4359%	14.0002%

Table 5.7 Required rate of return at the retirement age of 60 years

Length of services (Years)	*Life expectancy (years)*	*Contribution rate*						
		3%	*5%*	*7%*	*9%*	*10%*	*13%*	*15%*
10	75	69.2765%	60.7872%	55.3875%	51.4515%	49.8258%	45.8400%	43.7037%
	80	69.2781%	60.7906%	55.3933%	51.4602%	49.8361%	45.8557%	43.7234%
	85	69.2782%	60.7909%	55.3940%	51.4614%	49.8376%	45.8583%	43.7269%
	90	69.2782%	60.2617%	55.3941%	51.4615%	49.8378%	45.8587%	43.7275%
	95	69.2782%	60.7910%	55.3941%	51.4615%	49.8378%	45.8588%	43.7277%
20	75	35.0561%	31.5234%	29.2339%	27.5424%	26.8379%	25.0952%	24.1515%
	80	35.0729%	31.5498%	29.2694%	27.5868%	26.8866%	25.1564%	24.2208%
	85	35.0770%	31.5571%	29.2802%	27.6011%	26.9027%	25.1780%	24.2461%
	90	35.0780%	31.5592%	29.2835%	27.6057%	26.9081%	25.1857%	24.2555%
	95	35.0782%	31.5597%	29.2845%	27.6072%	26.9098%	25.1884%	24.2589%
30	75	24.5187%	22.3125%	20.8702%	19.7978%	19.3492%	18.2347%	17.6280%
	80	24.5643%	22.3736%	20.9442%	19.8832%	19.4399%	18.3400%	17.7422%
	85	24.5808%	22.3976%	20.9750%	19.9201%	19.4797%	18.3880%	17.7954%
	90	24.5869%	22.4072%	20.9879%	19.9362%	19.4975%	18.4104%	17.8208%
	95	24.5891%	22.4110%	20.9934%	19.9434%	19.5054%	18.4209%	17.8329%
40	75	18.7985%	17.1675%	16.0935%	15.2906%	14.9537%	14.1131%	13.6536%
	80	18.8884%	17.2773%	16.2190%	15.4293%	15.0983%	14.2738%	13.8239%
	85	18.9287%	17.3294%	16.2808%	15.4996%	15.1724%	14.3585%	13.9149%
	90	18.9470%	17.3547%	16.3120%	15.5360%	15.2113%	14.4043%	13.9649%
	95	18.9554%	17.3670%	16.3278%	15.5551%	15.2320%	14.4294%	13.9928%

Retirement Age Factor

Each country has a different pension structure for its retirement age. Malaysia's pension structure defines the pension age as mandatory when one has reached 55 years old. This mandatory age of 55 has been the practice for five decades until September 2001 (Moorthy et al., 2012). The mandatory retirement age was raised to 56 in October 2001. In 2021, with a retirement age set at 60 and a life expectancy of 80 years, each pensioner's payout had to last for almost 20 years. The mismatch has increased further due to a longer life expectancy, putting pressure on pension providers who risk longer and more uncertain post-retirement periods.

Figure 5.2 shows the retirement fund balance for the 55, 58, and 60 retirement age. Funding at the retirement age of 55 requires a higher return rate of 22.3905%. A higher return is due to sustaining a more extended post-retirement period of 25 years (80 years old minus 55 years at the time of retirement) compared to the retirement age of 58 years (22.3736%) and 60 years (22.3557%).

Contribution Rate Factor

The contribution rate is the percentage of the amount needed to be paid into the pension fund. In the Malaysian public service context, the contribution rate refers to how much the Malaysian government puts aside a certain amount of money for an individual's pension fund.

Figure 5.3 shows the retirement fund balance according to the contribution rate throughout the ten. Based on Fig. 5.3, only the 9% and 10% contributions were sustainable for funding a pensioner who retired at 60 and would die at 80 years old. However, the return was considered too optimistic by having 20% of the average rate of return. The result shows that a contribution of 9% would be sufficient for the scenario above. At the same time, contributions at 3%, 5%, and 7% were insufficient to support 20 years of post-retirement period with an assumption of 20% fund return. Hence, the fund balance scenario is as presented below:

Based on Table 5.8, assuming a 30% rate of return throughout the period, the minimum breakeven to cover this scenario is only 0.87% of the contribution rate. In comparison, a 25% of return will bring down the required contribution rate to 2.70%. The higher *Required Rate of*

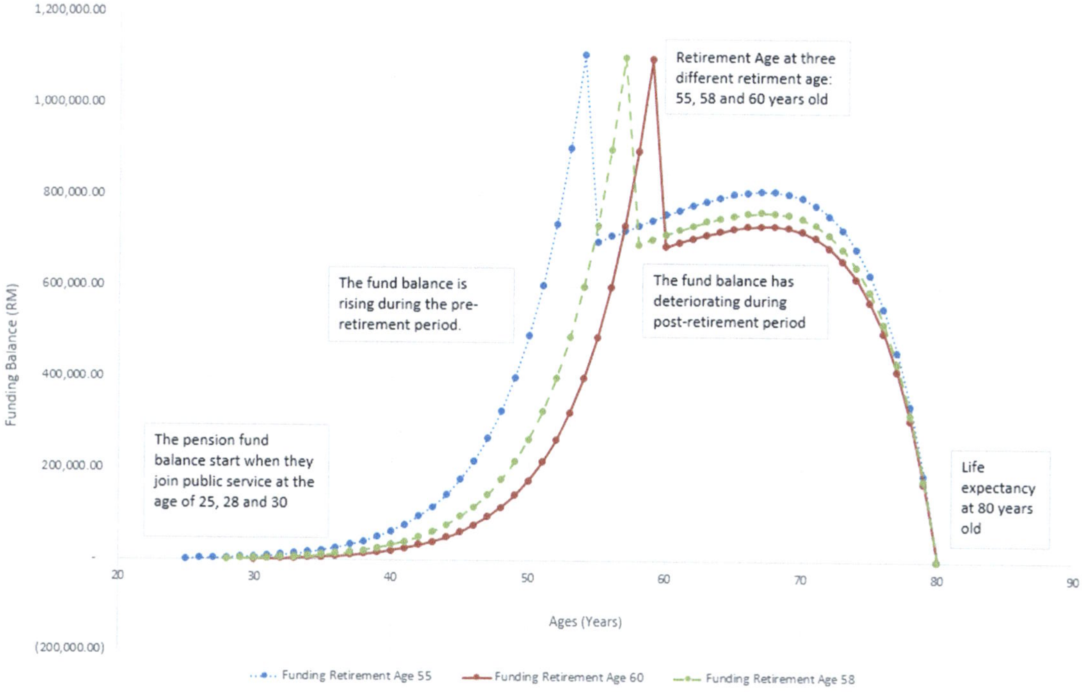

Fig. 5.2 Retirement fund balance according to retirement age (Constant Parameters: Life Expectancy—0 Years; Contribution Rate—%; and Length of Service—0 Years; *Note* Author's computation)

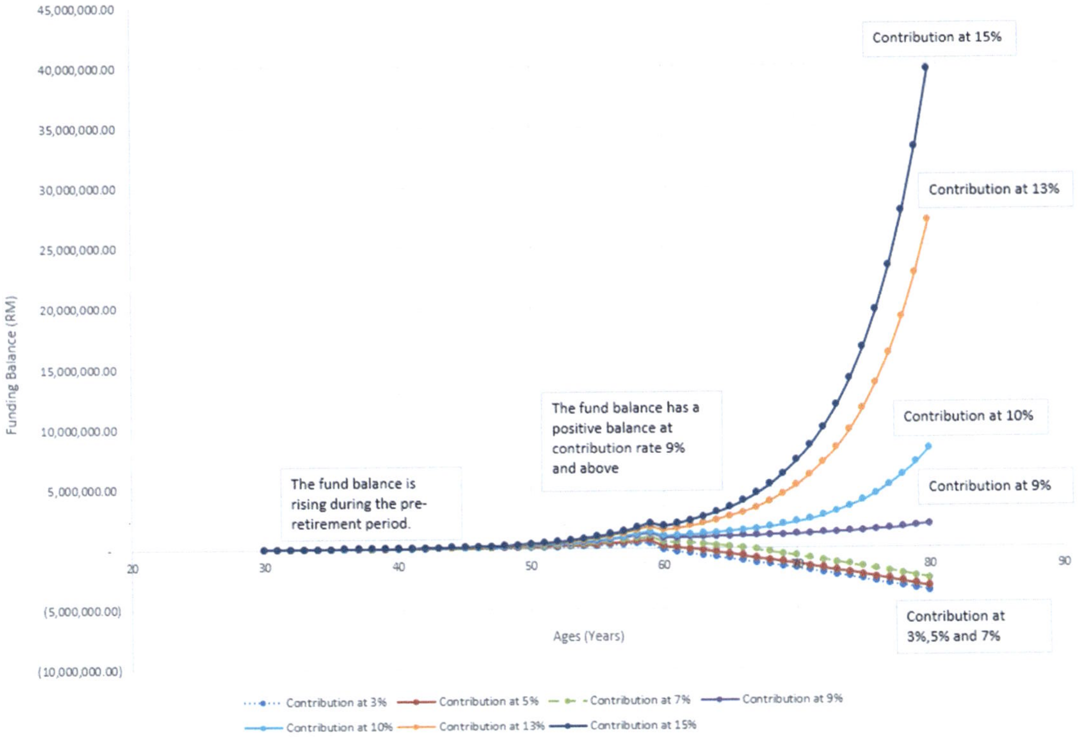

Fig. 5.3 Retirement fund balance according to the contribution rate (Constant Parameters: Life Expectancy is 80 Years; Retirement Age—is 60 Years; and Length of Service is 30 Years; Fund Rate of Return is 20%; *Note* Author's computation)

Table 5.8 Minimum contribution rate according to required rate of return

Required rate of return (%)	*Minimum contribution rate (%)*
30	0.87%
25	2.70%
20	8.70%
15	28.67%
10	95.41%
5	314.41%

Note Author's computation

Return will need a higher contribution rate. Table 5.8 proves that a higher required return is needed to sustain the lower contribution rate.

One of the main features of managing a pension fund is that the fund can pool investment risk across individuals and spread risk over a long tenure. Hence, the Malaysian government must balance the contribution rate and the expected investment return by the KWAP. Figure 5.4 shows how the contribution rate by the Malaysian government has a negative relationship with the required return. Since the Malaysian government pension provides an essential source of income to a civil servant in any contingency, the pension scheme is financially viable. Indeed, it must adequately finance to continue paying the expected benefits as has been stipulated in the pension laws in the future. However, the Malaysian government faces an increasing financial burden regarding the total pensions and gratuities payable.

Life Expectancy Factor

Figure 5.5 shows the retirement fund balance according to life expectancy. A higher life expectancy requires a higher rate of return on the fund.

Table 5.9 shows that the minimum required rate of return does not increase much if life expectancy increases by five years. However, the government needs to fund the retirement fund from its pocket higher than the minimum rate. This scenario illustrates the best-case scenario, where each increase in a variable should be supported by a higher contribution rate from the government.

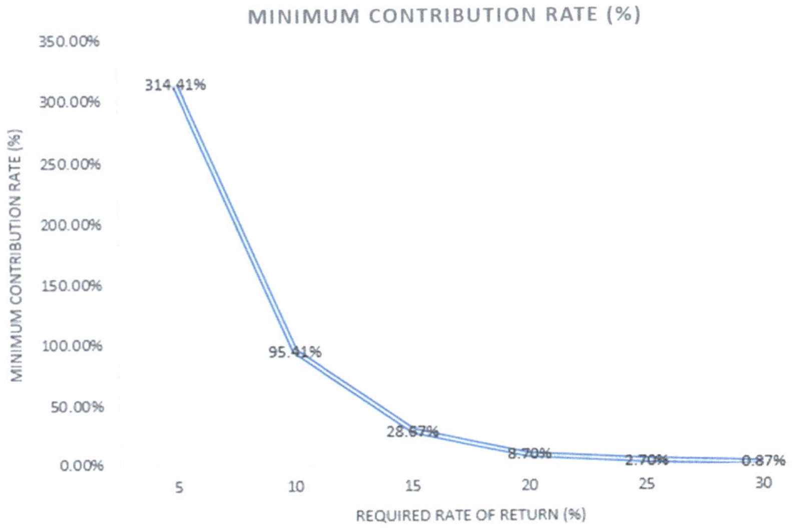

Fig. 5.4 Minimum contribution rate vs required rate of return (Constant Parameters: Retirement Age—60 Years; and Length of Service—30 Years; Life Expectancy—80 years; *Note* Author's computation)

Length of Service Factor

Figure 5.6 shows that long years of service result in a higher retirement fund balance. A higher fund balance will require a lower minimum return to generate profit in sustaining the plan for an extended period.

Regression Analysis

Based on the 560 scenarios generated, this study has run a regression analysis to model the required rate of return based on the independent variables.

Table 5.10 shows that Model (4) adequately explains the required return of the Malaysian Civil Servant Retirement Fund. About 84% variation of the required return can be explained by the contribution rate and length of service. The estimated Model is as follows:

$$\boldsymbol{RequiredReturn} = 0.6851 - 0.9559\boldsymbol{ContRate} - 0.0122\boldsymbol{Length}$$

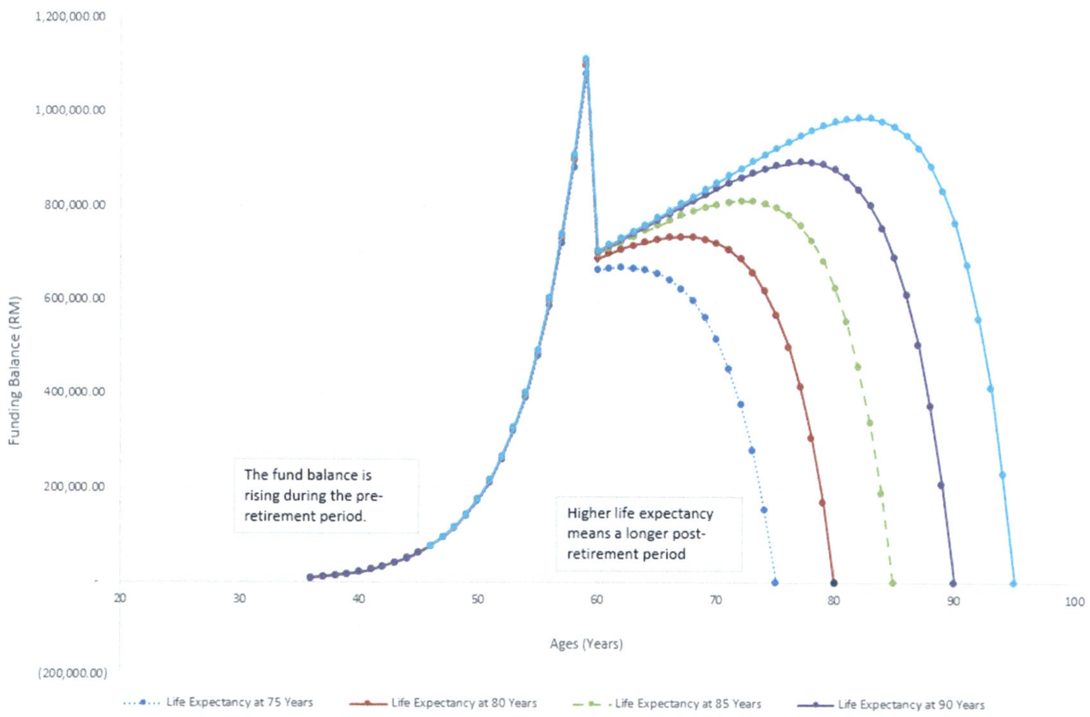

Fig. 5.5 Retirement fund balance according to life expectancy (Constant Parameters: Contribution Rate—5%; Retirement Age—60 Years; and Length of Service—30 Years; *Note* Author's computation)

Table 5.9 Minimum required rate of return according to life expectancy

Life expectancy (Years)	*Length of service/retired age (Years)*	*Contribution rate (%)*	*Required rate of return (%)*
75	30/60 Years	5.00	22.27
80			22.36
85			22.39
90			22.40
95			22.41

Note Author's computation

As shown in Table 5.11, H1 and H3 have supported the dependent variable, which is the required return of the fund. H_1 has stated that a higher contribution rate from the State and Federal governments to the KWAP pension fund enables the lower required return to be generated from the fund. H_3 reinforces the idea that there is a need for civil servants to work longer before they can enjoy pension benefits.

Table 5.12 shows the average required rate of return needed by the length of service and contribution rate. A future pensioner who worked for at least 30 years and above would push down the required return for the KWAP. For the final part of this study, a 5-year average gross return on investment (ROI) by the KWAP was used, and the trade-offs between the significant independent variables were computed as follows.

Table 5.13 and Table 5.14 show that the policymakers of the Post-Service Division need to work harder since it is impossible to contribute about 200–300% for each pensioner if the pensioners are expected to live until the age of 80 years old. If someone serves about ten years in the public sector, they are still eligible for the public pension fund. However, the government needs to contribute about 376% of the fund to the monthly payment payable to this pensioner during the person's retirement in the future. The current feature is not feasible since the government revenue is lower than the computed contribution rate. The number is generated based on the five-year average return of the KWAP fund between 2014 and 2018.

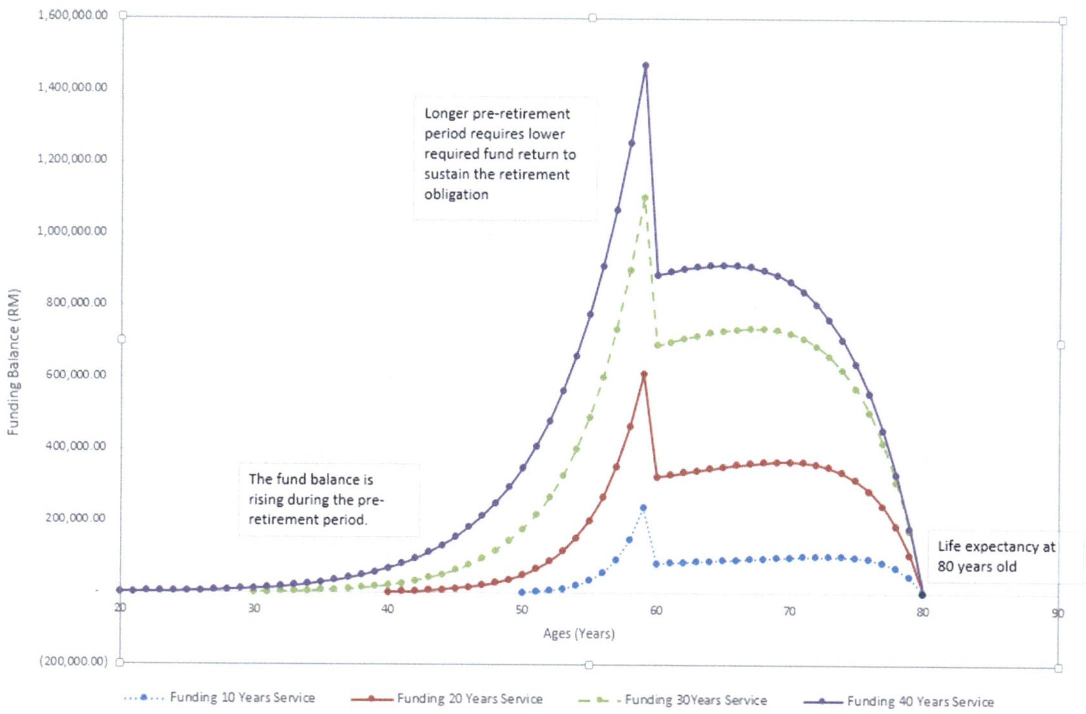

Fig. 5.6 Retirement fund balance according to the length of service (Constant Parameters: Contribution Rate—5%; Retirement Age—60; and Life Expectancy—80 Years; *Note* Author's computation)

Table 5.10 Regression analysis of the required rate of return

Independent variable	*Model: required return (dependent variable)*			
	(1)	*(2)*	*(3)*	*(4)*
ContRate (−)	−0.9559	−0.9559**	−0.9559**	−0.9559**
	(0.00)	(0.00)	(0.00)	(0.00)
LifeExp (+)	0.0001	–	0.0001	–
	(0.92)	–	(0.92)	–
Length (−)	−0.0121**	−0.0122**	−0.0121	−0.0122**
	(0.00)	(0.00)	(0.00)	(0.00)
RetiAge (−)	0.0001	−0.0000		–
	(0.98)	(0.98)		–
Constant	0.6840**	0.6872**	0.6820**	0.6851**
	(0.00)	(0.00)	(0.00)	(0.00)
Adjusted R-squared	0.8429	0.8432	0.8432	0.8435
F-statistic	751.03	1003.16	1003.18	15,007.44
Observations	560	560	560	560

Note Values in parenthesis are the *p*-values from the 560 scenarios generated. ** and * denote 1% and 5% levels of significance, respectively

Table 5.11 Summary of hypothesis test

Hypothesis	*Independent variable (Expected sign)*	*Required return*
H_1	Contribution Rate (−)	Supported
H_2	Life Expectancy (+)	–
H_3	Length of Service (−)	Supported
H_4	Retirement Age (−)	–

Table 5.12 Average required rate of return and contribution rate based on length of service

Length of Services (Years)	*Average Required Rate of Return / Contribution Rate*						
	3%	*5%*	*7%*	*9%*	*10%*	*13%*	*15%*
10	69.28%	60.68%	55.39%	51.46%	49.84%	45.85%	43.72%
20	35.07%	31.54%	29.26%	27.58%	26.88%	25.15%	24.21%
30	24.56%	22.37%	20.94%	19.88%	19.43%	18.33%	17.74%
40	18.90%	17.30%	16.25%	15.46%	15.13%	14.32%	13.87%

Table 5.13 5-year average Gross Return on Investment (ROI) by KWAP

Return on Investment (ROI) (%)/Year	*2014*	*2015*	*2026*	*2017*	*2018*	*Average*
Net	4.60	3.30	4.00	7.00	0.80	3.94
Gross	6.20	5.50	5.40	5.80	4.10	5.40

Table 5.14 Computed contribution rate based on average net and Gross ROI within five years: 3.94% (Net ROI) and 5.40% (Gross ROI)

Length of service (Years)	*Life expectancy/retired age (Years)*	*Contribution rate (%)*	
		Gross ROI	*Net ROI*
10	80/60 Years	375.28%	449.81%
20		326.60%	424.74%
30		286.04%	403.59%
40		202.40%	308.39%

5.4 Conclusion

Malaysia's rapidly increasing pension costs have raised serious concerns for policymakers and decision-makers. The result shows that the pre-retirement factors, such as the contribution rate and length of service, are more crucial in lowering the required rate of return. However, the post-retirement factors, such as the retirement age and life expectancy, are insignificant in determining the required rate of return.

The work-leisure model theory discusses the labour supply functions with a factor of leisure and wages that explain how long an individual should work in their career lifetime. Based on the theory, people will work if the wages exceed their needs and leisure. This theory also applies to Malaysia's public service labour supply.

The Malaysian government needs to fund the public sector retirement scheme higher than the current contribution rate of 5%. The government has considerable freedom to alter the contribution rate. However, the underlying principles of the amount contribution rate will depend on the surplus or deficit of the pension fund. The accumulated pension assets must be greater than the projected liabilities. Thus, in a sense, the contribution rate can be reduced during the period of surplus. In contrast, the contribution rate can be increased when the fund is in deficit. The flexibility may be restricted due to certain constraints in the fund.

As a policy suggestion, the government should introduce a few measures in the future. First, the government should reconsider the issue of pension eligibility based on the minimum years of service for a civil servant to be able to participate in the pension scheme. This study recommends that only those with a minimum of 20 years of service be eligible to participate in the pension scheme.

The KWAP pension fund needs 20 years before it is fully vested. The State becomes fully vested when the fund contributed by the State or Federal government is fully accessible by the pensioner or the beneficiary. Hence, those under 20 years of service should participate in the Employee Provident Fund (EPF).

According to the analysis carried out in this study, if an officer has only worked for ten years and joined the pension scheme, then the KWAP needs to generate a required return of more than 50% to sustain the pension benefits to the officer. On top of that, this study has found that extending the retirement age from 55 to 60 years does not reduce the required return significantly (see Tables 5.5 and 5.6). In addition, the length of service or year of contribution is more important than life expectancy in the post-retirement years.

Second, the government should set a minimum contribution rate even if the economy is in deficit. This study recommends a contribution rate of 13% based on the 648 simulated scenarios. The Federal government's current contribution rate of 5% to the KWAP is insufficient. Based on the current literature, there is a need for the Malaysian government to set a minimum funding ratio for the KWAP pension fund for its long-term sustainability.

Notes

1. "2013 Budget" accessed at http://www.jpapencen.gov.my/english/2012budget.html, accessed on 1 July 2021.
2. "2019 Malaysia Budget" accessed at https://www.mof.gov.my/arkib/revenue/2020/section3.pdf, accessed on 31 July 2021.

References

Abdul Rahman, M. I., & Lau, W.Y. (2023). Is the KWAP defined benefit pension fund sustainable in the long run? *International Journal of Banking and Finance, 18*(2), 97–126. https://doi.org/10.32890/ijbf2023.18.2.5

Alestalo, N., & Puttonen, V. (2006). Asset allocation in Finnish pension funds. *Journal of Pension Economics and Finance, 5*(1), 27–44. https://doi.org/10.1017/S1474747205002295

Ambachtsheer, K. P. (1994). The economics of pension fund management. *Financial Analysts Journal, 50*(6), 21–31. https://doi.org/10.2469/faj.v50.n6.21

Barr, N., & Diamond, P. (2006). The economics of pensions. *Oxford Review of Economic Policy, 22*(1), 15–39. https://doi.org/10.1093/oxrep/grj002

Barr, N., & Diamond, P. (2009). Reforming pensions: Principles, analytical errors and policy directions. *International Social Security Review, 62*(2), 5–29. https://doi.org/10.1111/j.1468-246X.2009.01327.x

Blake, D., Lehmann, B. N., & Timmermann, A. (1999). Asset allocation dynamics and pension fund performance. *Journal of Business, 72*(4), 429–461. https://doi.org/10.1086/209623

Chernoff, J. (2003). Asset liability management back with a twist. *Pensions and Investments*. Retrieved from https://www.pionline.com/article/20030721C/PRINT/307210719/asset-liability-management-back-with-a-twist

Holzmann, R., Palacios, R., & Zviniene, A. (2004). *Implicit pension debt: issues, measurement and scope in international perspective. 0403*, 38. http://documents.worldbank.org/curated/en/947731468762352221/Implicit-pension-debt-issues-measurement-and-scope-in-international-perspective

Jidwin, A. P., Ali, R., & Tuyon, J. (2012). The Malaysian employees provident fund's members' investment scheme: Survey of fund selection, performance and perceptions. *Management, 1*(9), 31–43.

JPA. (2021). *Malaysia pension scheme*. Bahagian Pasca Perkhidmatan. http://www.jpapencen.gov.my/english/pension_scheme.html

KWAP. (2018). KWAP Annual Report 2018. *KWAP Website, 86*(3), 64–65. https://www.kwap.gov.my/EN/UsefulInformation/Publication/AnnualReports/KWAP Annual Report 2018.pdf

Lee, K. C. (1997). The Malaysian government pension scheme. Whither is its future direction? *Jurnal Ekonomi Malaysia, 31*, 87–106.

Martell, C. R., Kioko, S. N., & Moldogaziev, T. (2013). Impact of unfunded pension obligations on the credit quality of state governments. *Public Budgeting and Finance, 33*(3), 24–54. https://doi.org/10.1111/j.1540-5850.2013.12013.x

Ministry of Finance Malaysia (MOF). (2019). Malaysia 2020 Budget Speech by YB Tuan Lim Guan Eng. Parliament Malaysia, October 2019, 1–13.

Moorthy, M. K., Durai, T., Chelliah, L., Sien, C. S., Leong, L. C., Kai, N. Z., Rhu, W. C., & Teng, W. Y. (2012). A study on the retirement planning behaviour of working individuals in Malaysia. *International Journal of Academic Research in Economics and Management Sciences, 1*(2), 54.

Munnell, A. H., Aubry, J. P., & Quinby, L. (2011a). Public pension funding in practice. *Journal of Pension Economics and Finance, 10*(2), 247–268. https://doi.org/10.1017/S1474747211000126

OECD. (2020). Pension Funds in Figures 2020. *OECD, June*, 1–5. Retrieved from https://www.oecd.org/pensions/Pension-Funds-in-Figures-2020.pdf

Papke, L. E. (1991). *The asset allocation of private pension plans*. National Bureau of Economic Research

Rudolf, M., & Ziemba, W. T. (2004). Intertemporal Surplus Management. *Journal of Economic Dynamics and Control, 28*(5), 975–990. https://doi.org/10.1016/S0165-1889(03)00058-7

Warr, P. (1987). *Work, unemployment, and mental health*. Oxford University Press.

CHAPTER 6

Can Longevity Bonds Mitigate the Longevity Risk of the Pension Scheme?

6.1 Introduction

Due to advancements in health care, life expectancy is expected to increase in years to come. The projection from the Department of Statistics Malaysia (DOSM) shows that the number of Malaysians aged 60 years and above will increase from 2.3 million (8.2% of the population) in 2010 to 5.5 million (14.4% of the population) in 2030. The elderly Malaysians will have inadequate savings due to extended life expectancy, resulting from shorter years of savings to prepare for a longer post-retirement period.

Another study by Yew and Cheong (2013) suggested that family support is weakening as the primary care for older people in Malaysia. Their study discusses numerous difficulties brought on by the ageing population, whether personal, family, or societal. People experience various health problems as they age and must change their lifestyles and habits. These people, who are older family members, need long-term care, which increases the financial strain on those who are employed.

The ageing society implies that a higher budget allocation for health-care services and infrastructure by the government is needed. In addition, the government must also consider sustaining public pension liabilities as pensioners are expected to live longer during the post-retirement period. A higher obligation will affect the willingness and ability of pension providers to keep providing an annuity to pensioners in the future. In the case of Malaysia, the government still must continue to provide pension

M. I. Abdul Rahman and W. Y. Lau, *Pension at Stake*,
https://doi.org/10.1007/978-981-97-2324-9_6

payments to the dependents even after the pensioner's death. The longer life expectancy will translate into more longevity risk for the defined benefit pension scheme provider.

In Malaysia, the State and Federal governments' annual contribution to Retirement Fund Incorporated (KWAP) funds the public employee pension scheme. There is an ongoing issue that the pension cost has increased over many years. The retirement cost in the 2019 and 2020 Federal Budget stood at 27.06 and 27.12 billion of the operating expenditure (OPEX), respectively. The Malaysian government needs to consider an alternative instrument to reduce the burden while maintaining the current scheme.

Longevity risk affects private companies, insurance companies, annuity providers, and even the government in managing pension funds for a group of civil servants. In terms of government, an ageing population demands more financial resources, policies, infrastructure, and workforce to support this group longer. At the same time, Hussein (2019) believed this situation requires the government to provide better healthcare and social protection to the poor and elderly.

Cairns (2013) believed the pension fund is one of the most publicised industries impacted by rising longevity. Hence, it is critical to discuss an idea to hedge this risk. In the meantime, the insurance industry also faces challenges due to increased longevity. The pension provider plans to buy annuities from or sell their liabilities to reinsurers and insurers to purchase reinsurance. However, due to the longevity risk, annuity and pension providers' costs tend to be higher. The price can be lower if the provider can hedge the longevity risk since they do not have to bear the cost.

It is essential for the parties involved to leverage the market movement. Since the market has always risen and gone down, the players shall be more flexible in adopting investment strategies to bring down the cost to the pension provider. Besides, there is a regulatory requirement factor for some countries. For example, Cairns (2013) stated that the Solvency II directive becomes a measure to evaluate longevity risk for the insurance industries under the new European regulatory environment. It proves the need for longevity risk management solutions to transfer longevity risks to reinsurers and financial markets.

Blake (2018) also discussed how to deal with longevity risk. First, the party must accept longevity risk as a legitimate business risk, so earning a longevity index premium to cover or net off the longevity risk is possible.

Second, longevity risk can be shared, while third, reinsurance can be utilised to lay off longevity-linked products/securities. Finally, the risk of longevity-linked products can be managed or securitised; as Blake (2018) mentioned, the last two options must be carried out in the "Life Market".—The market is related to the transfer of longevity and mortality risks.

In this respect, a longevity risk term structure will help regulators calculate any risks levied to the government-linked pension funds, such as those administrated by the US Pension Benefit Guaranty Corporation and the UK Pension Protection Fund. In the private sector, sponsors of the defined benefit retirement plans shall be able to reduce longevity risks. The ability to hedge longevity would reduce insurers' capital requirements, a relevant aspect to consider should increase the demand for annuities. Moreover, longevity bonds would reduce the concentration of longevity risk among insurers by spreading the longevity risk around the capital markets.

Based on the above literature, this study proposes using longevity bonds as one of the solutions for the Defined Benefit Pension System in Malaysia. The remaining part of this chapter is arranged as follows. Section two reviews the literature, followed by a discussion on methodology and an outline of how the longevity bond can be introduced under the Malaysian capital market. The last section concludes our study.

6.2 Longevity Risk

Uncertainty about how far humans can survive is a longevity risk. This risk is when the basis of holistic social protection for the ageing population is broader as the working-age group shrinks (Yew & Cheong, 2013). In addition, Rappaport and Parikh (2002) argued that longevity had changed the balance between service providers and retirees who keep consuming the resources. Hence, many have suggested that the government raise the compulsory retirement age to maintain this balance as the population ages. Besides, the longer life expectancy worldwide affects all pension schemes globally.

Blake (2018) discussed that longevity risk consists of a few components. In addition to the longevity risk trend, specific longevity risk refers to idiosyncratic and modelling risks. Idiosyncratic risk is brought by a situation where individuals from the same population of interest have different lengths of time. Meanwhile, modelling risk means other models will project different lifetimes for these individuals. These risks (idiosyncratic and modelling) get diversified in a sufficiently large population of interest.

In short, longevity risk has expanded in Eq. (6.1) as follows:

$$\begin{aligned} Longevity\ Risk = Trend\ Risk + [&sum\ of\ idiosyncratic\ risk \\ &+ modelling\ risk] \end{aligned} \tag{6.1}$$

6.3 The Life Market

A promising global capital market is now trading longevity-index assets and liabilities related to changes in human life expectancy, known as the "Life Market". The longevity of supply and demand make up the life market. Longevity suppliers are the entities that hold longevity risks and want to offload the risk. Hence, they are looking to buy protection from the investors. The literature has suggested two entities with a long supply of longevity risk. For instance, pharmaceutical companies that provide medicine for older people and elderly care homes provide long-term services to take care of older people.

Meanwhile, the investor is an entity that takes longevity risk and receives a risk premium as has been promised to them. Blake (2018) mentioned that short-term investors might be interested in the market with sufficient liquidity to protect their interests. However, to buy protection from investors, the supplier does consider a basis risk when ineffective hedging happens.

Mortality is deemed as a stochastic process. Suppliers come from DB plans, annuity providers, pension measures, and reinsurances. For investors, there are two types: the insurance market and the capital market, known as the life market (for the medium- and long-term market). For the insurance market, life insurers and reinsurance are involved. The capital market comprises a few entities, such as Insurance-Linked Securities (ILS) funds and other hedge funds and investors. These investors seek a lower correlation with traditional assets such as equity and bonds.

Blake (2018) highlighted that one of the attractions of longevity-linked assets is that they are uncorrelated with traditional financial assets such as equities and bonds. The feature can be used to further diversify the investment portfolio. Hence, risk reduction is a benefit for investors in choosing any life market assets. Blake et al. (2019) explained risk reduction benefits from a pension fund, even having a small allocation to a longevity-linked asset. However, it is crucial to note that there shall be some smaller second-order correlations. When it comes to credit risk, when investors of an insurance company are involved in counterparty risk, liquidity, and interest rate risk, the investors shall use funding and leverage through economic linkages, both in the short term and long term.

6.4 The Capital Market Hedging

Capital market hedging is valued from two angles. Blake et al. (2019) state that the first is to minimise the longevity risk. However, risk minimisation may not be preferred when a hedger cares about the overall longevity risk profile.

The second angle is sensitivity matching. It involves the sensitivity of the hedged liabilities and the hedging instruments used to change the underlying mortality. Rather than focusing on specific objectives, it tries to replicate a portfolio similar to the liability hedged in terms of longevity risk. Exposure is more flexible than risk minimisation—since mortality sensitivity measures can be applied to life contingency liability and mortality derivatives.

From an investor's perspective, standardised products such as swaps and forwards shall be regularly offered in the market. However, the standardisation of hedging instruments does not eliminate the risk (Coughlan et al., 2010). In the capital markets, investors demand transparency and liquidity. Hence, there is a need for custom-made hedging instruments to be introduced in the market.

Regarding hedging strategies, Yang et al. (2019) deliberated three methods: natural, external, and a mix of natural and external hedging. As a result, a combination of internal and external hedging strategies is the most effective in managing longevity risk. The researcher and investors shall consider that risk reduction will increase the hedge's effectiveness.

First, Yang et al. (2019) explained that natural hedging occurs when insurers hedge the longevity risk using their products, such as life insurance and annuity because they are sensitive in opposing ways in changing the mortality rate.

Second, regarding external hedging, life insurance and pension providers can use capital market alternatives to mitigate longevity risk. In recent studies, the capital market has been utilised to transfer longevity risk via securitisation of longevity risk. Besides, various survivor securities and derivatives are developed in academics and practice. Blake et al. (2014) stated that the annuity markets had facilitated the emergence of a traded market in the longevity-linked capital market instruments. Blake and Burrows (2007) first proposed that issuing survivor bonds can help pension funds insure against longevity risk.

There is a discussion regarding the advantages and disadvantages of the longevity hedger's internal and external hedging strategies. Lin and Cox (2005) suggested that natural hedging is a good strategy for internal hedging. However, it may be costly in internal life insurance and annuity products. This strategy could drive the insurers to exploit natural hedging using mortality swaps to enable a lower risk premium charge than others.

In addition, the restriction in utilising the natural hedging strategy has led insurers to adjust the sales volume of life insurance and annuity products to maintain an optimal liability proportion, which is sometimes not feasible in industry practice.

6.5 Basis Risk and Hedging Effectiveness

The idea between the population associated with the pension plan or annuity portfolio is known as the "exposed population", and the population related to the hedging instrument is known as the "hedging population". Hence, hedging effectiveness is a relative comparison between the exposed and the hedging populations (Li et al., 2019). Basis risk is a mismatch between the underlying hedged and hedging instruments. It also means that the index mortality experience will differ from the pension plan. Then, the hedge shall be imperfect, thus increasing the residual risk. Perfect hedging produces a minimum basis risk. The presence of basis risk in hedging renders the hedging implementation less effective.

The presence of basis risk means that hedge effectiveness will be imperfect and that, upon implementation, the hedged position shall still have some residual risk. Hedging effectiveness is affected by mismatches, be it the cash flow timing or differences in variables that determine cash flow. Hence, the increase in basis risk reduces the hedging effectiveness level. It implies that lower basis risk indicates "good" hedging. Therefore, a "good" hedge is a situation in which the basis risk is small relative to the risk of the initial unhedged position. Li and Hardy (2012) argued that the basis risk could be minimised via careful structuring and calibration of the hedging instrument.

Li and Hardy (2012) explained that demographic terms measure basis risk while economic terms measure effectiveness to calibrate the basis risk. They added that the effectiveness is determined by focusing on the degree of risk reduction in economic terms using the Morte-Carlo simulation. It helps generate various mortality rate situations for exposed and hedging populations.

In longevity and mortality, basis risk is often related to demographic mismatches between the "exposed population" and the "hedging population" associated with the hedging instrument. The demographic mismatches arise because these two populations are completely different; one is a subpopulation or because of differences in just a few individuals. Such mismatches can be classified according to minor demographic characteristics such as gender, age, socioeconomic class, or geographical location (Richards & Jones, 2004).

Li and Hardy (2012) believed that socioeconomic is a crucial determinant for index-based hedging situations. For instance, the "gender-bias" mismatch, the mismatch between mortality of different ages ("age basis"), the mismatch between "subpopulation basis", and even country basis can be minimised by structuring the hedging instrument. One would expect a more negligible basis risk if the two populations have similar characteristics. On the other hand, the risk could be significant if the two populations have different profiles, but this is not necessarily the case. Certainly, Liu and Li (2018) explained that the longevity basis risk reduces the effectiveness of longevity hedging. However, the relationship between these two is not as straightforward as one might suppose.

The crucial factor in assessing hedge effectiveness is to start from hedging objectives to reflect the nature of the risk being hedged and focus on the degree of risk reduction in economic terms.

6.6 Hedging Method

Hedging longevity risk with index-based instruments is helpful for several reasons. First, Cairns et al. (2008) discuss standardising the longevity exposure to reflect the index, and there is potential to create greater liquidity and lower hedging costs. Furthermore, second, pension plans are too large to hedge the full extent of their longevity exposure. Hence, the literature suggested three main hedging methods used in the market: q-forward, survivor swap, and longevity bond.

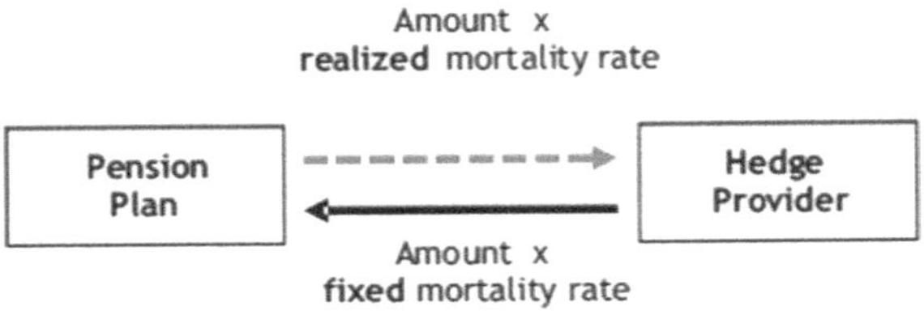

Fig. 6.1 Q-forward swap on the mortality rate

Method of Hedging 1: Q-forward

A mortality forward rate contract also refers to the "q-forward" contract because the letter "q" is the standard actuarial symbol for mortality rate. This hedging instrument is the most straightforward instrument to transfer longevity (mortality) risk. The product works by involving a contract between two parties. They agree to exchange an amount proportional to a given population that has realised mortality rate or subpopulations. Chuang and Brockett (2014) stated that in return for that payment, the amount proportional to a fixed mortality rate agreed during the inception will be payable at future dates until the contract maturity.

The first capital market derivative to be executed was in January 2008 by Lucida as the hedger and J.P. Morgan as the hedge provider. The payments are linked to the LifeMetrics index based on the mortality of males of different ages in England and Wales. Figure 6.1 shows the "q-forward" exchanges fixed mortality for realised mortality at the contract maturity.

Hedging longevity risk of a pension plan via the q-forward works by receiving the fixed mortality rate (issuer) and paying the realised mortality rate at the end of the contract. This approach will enable the pension plan provider to lock the mortality rate in the future as it needs to pay whatever amount according to the actual rates at the current dates. The counterparty in this transaction, such as an investment bank, has the opposite exposure: to pay the fixed mortality rate and receive the realised rate.

Method of Hedging 2: Longevity (or Survivor) Swap

A longevity swap, also known as a survivor swap, is a swap instrument used by the capital market hedger. This instrument exchanges actual pension payments for a series of pre-agreed fixed payments. Each exchange payment will be based on the weighted real survival rate.

In April 2007, the Swiss Re and Friends' Provident announced the world's first swap. It is a pure longevity risk transfer in the form of an insurance contract instead of a capital market instrument. The swap was based on a £1.7 billion book of 78,000 pension annuity contracts by Friends' Provident between July 2001 and December 2006. Indeed, Swiss Re makes payments and assumes longevity risk for an undisclosed premium.

In July 2008, the J.P. Morgan-Canada Life longevity swap, the world's first capital market longevity swap, was announced. Canada Life's hedged annuity value amounted to £500 m, representing 125,000 lives using a 40-year swap customised to the insurer's longevity exposure (Blake, 2018). The aim is to transfer the longevity risk to the investors, as J.P. Morgan acted as the intermediary counterparty.

Method of Hedging 3: Longevity Bond

In managing the uncertainty of life expectancy, market players have developed financial bond instruments to fix the population's longevity. One is the longevity bond, a fixed-income product designed to transfer the risk to other entities. A longevity bond is a type of security that hedges against entities exposed to longevity risks, such as the government that provides defined benefits, insurance companies, and annuity providers. The idea behind this security is to have increased payment as the hedging population lives longer than expected in the future. Using this instrument, the government can transfer the risk to entities that demand longevity risk, such as investors.

The first longevity bond was issued in November 2004 by the European Investment Bank. However, the lead arranger of the idea is BNP Paribas, along with PartnerRe Ltd. This global reinsurance company acts as the longevity risk reinsurer. The issue size of this first bond was £540 million, which matures within 25 years from the issuance date, and the initial coupon is £50 million. The future coupon payments are linked to the mortality index of 65-year-old males from England and Wales. However, there is no return of principal after 25 years old.

This bond was initially targeted at the United Kingdom (UK) pension funds. It would hedge against the systematic longevity risk faced by the pension at that time. However, the bond issuance has failed to attract sufficient investors and then withdrawn from the market.

Nevertheless, the Swiss Re mortality catastrophe bond launched in December 2003 was more successful. This product is aimed to enable the issuer to reduce its exposure to catastrophic mortality events, such as a severe influenza outbreak, a major terrorist attack (using weapons of mass destruction), or even a natural catastrophe. The bond, known as VITA 1, was issued as a 3-year contract that matures on 1st January 2007.

Furthermore, the Swiss Re longevity spread bond, known as the Kortis bond, was issued in December 2010, seven years after issuing the catastrophe bond in 2003. The issue size is $50 million, and the tenure is eight years. The investors would hold the bond that is exposed to the risk of any increase in the longevity divergence index value (LDIV) spread of the annualised mortality improvement between the males aged from 75 to 85 years old in Great Britain and Wales versus males aged from 55 to 85 years old in the US. The purpose of the bond is to hedge the Swiss Re's exposure to longevity risk faced by the issuer. The bond is designed under the principal-at-risk concept. These are examples of how fixed-income products help in hedging risk exposure.

Blake et al. (2010) highlighted that most longevity bonds might not involve principal repayment. Instead, it shall apply a coupon linked to the survivor cohort. However, Blake et al. (2014) explained that the coupon for longevity bonds is purely based on the "survivorship" of a hedging population. As the mortality rate of a hedging population increases, coupon payment drops until it eventually reaches zero since the mortality rate and coupon rate have an inversely proportional relationship.

Blake et al. (2011) proposed a longevity bond with coupons based on the difference between the realised survivors and expected survivors of a specific cohort. At the same time, Blake et al. (2014) stated that the government has the advantage of sharing the longevity risk via the longevity bond instrument. First, it is interested in ensuring an efficient annuity market for longevity risk transfers and the best instrument for intergenerational risk-sharing.

Mortality-linked derivatives have high demand in developed markets. The product resembles longevity bonds but is significantly different as it uses mortality rates, while longevity bonds use survivor rates. Blake et al. (2014) suggested that the government consider tail risk hedging (population above 90 and 95 years old) using a longevity index bond.

However, Thomsen et al. (2007) disclosed the problems related to longevity bonds. In general, the market is short of demand to cover investors. Besides, some externalities may hinder the development market itself. The market growth may increase once the volume has passed the critical market level.

In the end, the government shall promote an efficient annuity market to safeguard the solvency and liquidity of the market players to spread the longevity risk. International entities such as the International Monetary Fund (IMF) and the Organisation for Economic Cooperation and Development (OECD) have recognised few government initiatives in the longevity bond market.

Blake and Burrows (2007) also suggested that the government can improve the market instead of private entities by producing a longevity index and coupon payment. The government can provide longevity bond pricing benchmarks and liquidity by introducing the number of survivors. Then, any future bond coupon payment shall depend on the percentage of survivors surviving the coupon payment dates. However, Blommestein (2006) argued that this idea might cause a problem when the product is heavily exposed to the risk.

Instead of the government acting as the issuer, Blake et al. (2014) believed private sector organisations could also issue longevity bonds. The studies suggested that pharmaceutical companies issue longevity bonds as their revenue is positively associated with survivorship. The pharmaceutical sectors are always long on longevity risk. Blake et al. (2010) said that the theory might be correct. However, the demand for longevity bonds is far higher than the conceivable supply from such companies.

However, the government needs to deliberate before engaging in this instrument. Antolin and Blommestein (2007) proposed that any government anticipate the equilibrium effect of aggregate instead of individual risks. Antolin and Blommestein (2007) mentioned that the pension promised by the government to the current pensioners should be higher than expected since it will pay out the periodic gratuities in a lump sum. Public policies' role in sharing longevity risk depends on the individual and aggregate longevity risk differences. Antolin and Blommestein (2007) stated that the micro-longevity risk (survival risk) could be solved efficiently via the annuity market.

6.7 Methodology

Basis Risk and Hedging Effectiveness

A bond or fixed income is a financial instrument in which the borrower or issuer must fulfil a fixed payment amount on a fixed schedule. Hence, the borrower makes a uniform payment to investors using a coupon throughout the tenure.

Longevity Bond

Lin and Cox (2005) suggested that a longevity bond pays coupons based on the difference between a given cohort's realised and expected survivors. The cash flows of the coupon bond contract are defined as follows:

Consider an annuity or pension provider initially paying immediate annuities to a cohort of lx0 annuitants, all aged × 0. Let R be the annual payment of the individual annuity, and $l_{x0+\ t}$ denotes the number of survivors to age $_{x0+\ t}$ for t = 1, 2, 3, 4, 5, and so on.

The annuity provider will pay R (lx0 + t) within a time, where $l_{x0+\ t}$ is a random value at evaluation time t = 0.

However, given the expected number of $l_{x0+\ t}$ to age x + t, the annuity provider is exposed to the risk of systematic deviations between the $l_{x0+\ t}$ and the expected $l_{x0+\ t}$ at each time of T. The differences between the expected and real survivors represent the losses experienced by the annuity provider at each time of T. Then, such losses can be hedged through securitisation.

Given that SPC buys, at the price of W, a straight coupon bond with annual coupon R*C and principal R*F shall be refunded at maturity t = T. Let P be the premium that the annuity provider pays to SPC to hedge its longevity risk and V the price paid by the investors to purchase the longevity bond issued from SPC with the R*F value and coupons R*D. The structure of such transactions is shown in Fig. 6.2. Thus, SPC meets its obligation and gets a P + V > W profit.

As illustrated in Fig. 6.2, the Coupon for a Longevity Bond is based on the premium paid by the Annuity Provider and the Price paid by Investors. Compared to the straight bond with the maturity of T, the aggregate cash flow RCt shall be paid at each time t, and the principal RF upon the maturity, T. However, the special purpose vehicle (SPV) company will split the coupon between the annuity provider and investors

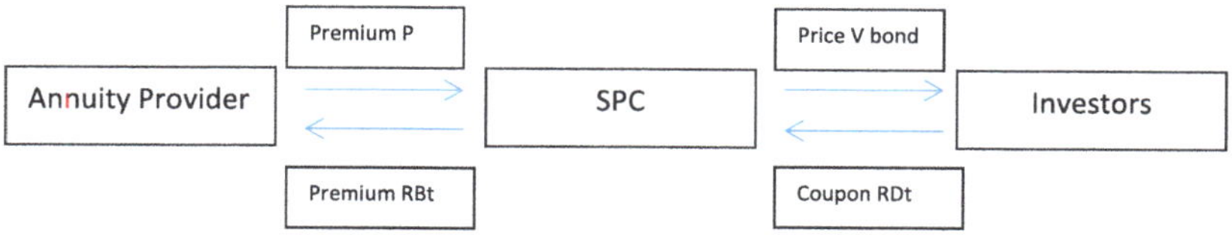

Fig. 6.2 Longevity bond cash flow illustration

into financial instruments, depending on the realised mortality at each time (t = 1, 2, 3, ... T). Hence, the formula for each longevity bond coupon is illustrated by Eq. (6.2) as follows:

$$R_{Ct} = R_{Bt} + R_{Dt} \tag{6.2}$$

Every coupon payment made by the annual provider consists of the following:

1. RBt represents the benefits received by the annuity provider used to cover the experienced loss up to the maximum level of RCt and
2. RDt is the payments received by the investors.

Note that R_{Dt} is specific to the payments R_{Bt}.

Equation (6.3) assumes a longevity bond with the constant fixed coupons RC. The benefits received by the annuity provider are RBt, where Bt is equal to:

$$R_{Bt} = \begin{cases} C \\ I_{X0+t} - E(I_{X0=t}) \\ 0 \end{cases} \tag{6.3}$$

Condition 1: The condition for the payment RBt is as follows:

$$R_{Bt} = C, \; when \; I_{X0+t} - E(I_{X0+t}) > C \tag{6.4}$$

Equation (6.4) illustrates the condition where the annuity provider shall receive the coupon rate when the expected life expectancy for each tenure is higher than the coupon rate. When the differences in life expectancy are lesser than the coupon rate, the annuity provider will receive a different amount, as in Eq. (6.5).

$$R_{Bt} = I_{X0+t} - E(I_{X0+t})\,When\,0 < I_{X0+t} - E(I_{X0+t}) \leq C \tag{6.5}$$

Condition 2: The annuity provider shall get zero payment if any of the cohort life expectancies are lower than the expected rate, as follows in Eq. (6.6):

$$R_{Bt} = 0\,When\,I_{X0+t} - E(I_{X0+t}) \leq 0 \tag{6.6}$$

Compared to RBt, the payments to the investors are RDt, where Dt is equal to Eq. (6.7):

$$R_{Dt} = \begin{cases} C \\ I_{X0+t} - E(I_{X0=t}) \\ C \end{cases} \tag{6.7}$$

The condition for the payment Rbt is as follows:

$$R_{Dt} = 0,\ when\,I_{X0+t} - E(I_{X0+t}) > C \tag{6.8}$$

The annuity provider will receive the coupon rate, as stated in Eq. (6.8), when the expected life expectancy for each tenure exceeds the coupon rate. When the differences in life expectancy are less than the coupon rate, the annuity provider will receive a different amount, as in Eq. (6.9).

$$R_{Dt} = I_{X0+t} - E(I_{X0+t})\,When\,0 < I_{X0+t} - E(I_{X0+t}) \leq C \tag{6.9}$$

Condition 3: The annuity provider will get payment zero if any of the cohort life expectancies are lower than the expected rate, as follows in Eq. (6.10):

$$R_{Bt} = C\,when\,I_{X0+t} - E(I_{X0+t}) \leq 0 \tag{6.10}$$

It means SPC will pay for two coupons. One benefit is for the annuity provider, while another is for the investors. Hence, the longevity bond's coupon payment according to the situation is summarised in Table 6.1.

The annuity provider's payout at time t from 0 depends on $l_{x0+\ t}$. In contrast, premiums paid by any annuitants of the cohort depend on the expected cash flows from the expected $l_{x0+\ t}$. Therefore, before the

Table 6.1 Summary of cash flow of longevity bond

Situation	*Equation*	*Annuity Provider (Rbt)*	*Investor (Rdt)*
Different Life Expectancy is less than zero	$I_{X0+t} - E(I_{X0+t}) \leq 0$	Zero	Receive full longevity bond coupon
Different Life Expectancy between Zero and Coupons	$0 < I_{X0+t} - E(I_{X0+t}) \leq C$	The annuity provider will receive the differences between expected life expectancy and real expectancy	The investor will receive the differences between expected life expectancy and real expectancy
Different Life Expectancy is more than a coupon	$I_{X0+t} - E(I_{X0+t}) > C$	The annuity provider will receive the coupon payment	The investor will receive zero

longevity bond is bought, the random loss experienced by the annuity provider at time t is as follows in Eq. (6.11):

$$Loss_t = R\,(I_{X0+t} - E(I_{X0+t}) \tag{6.11}$$

Equation (6.12) illustrates that once the longevity bond is bought, the Equation of losses is:

$$Loss_t = Loss_t - R_{bT} \tag{6.12}$$

6.8 Simulation of the Malaysian Longevity Bond

The life-abridged table is retrieved from the Department of Statistics Malaysia (DOSM). The expected life expectancy is compared to the one provided. In this study, we define that life expectancy (number of survivors) I_{X0+t} is based on the Department of Statistics (DOSM) life arbitraged and expectancy life expectancy (number of survivors) $E(I_{X0+t})$ is based on life arbitrage from the World Health Organisation (WHO) (2020).

The bond simulation details are as below:

Face Value (RM)	1,000,000,000	At the start of the longevity bond in Malaysia, an issuance size of RM1 billion was sufficient to attract more investors in helping the Malaysia government to hedge the longevity risk for the Defined Benefit
Coupon (%)	5%	Suggested coupons to attract new investors in the market
Tenure	20 Years	An average bond issued in Malaysia is twenty years, and the extended maturity date will attract more investors, such as insurance-linked companies
Issue Date	The cohort at given 40 years old	An average Malaysian becomes a civil servant at 30 years old. As ruled by the Pension Department under JPA, there are ten years of probation periods before the pension benefit is fully vested
Exposed Population	l_{X0+t}	The number of survivors for an exposed population is derived from the Life Arbitrage Table by the Department of Statistics Malaysia (DOSM)
Hedging Population	$E(l_{X0+t})$	The number of survivors for the hedging population (reference population) is derived from the Life Arbitrage Table by the World Health Organisation (WHO)
Year	2020, 2015, 2010	

6.9 Analysis

Three parties shall be considered for the Malaysian civil servant pension scheme.

The Issuer of the Longevity Bond

The government is the most appropriate party to issue such a bond of the required volume (Blake et al., 2010). The government is interested in promoting an efficient and well-functioning capital market while safeguarding the solvency of insurance companies. Besides, international organisations such as the International Monetary Fund (IMF) and the Organisation for Economic Cooperation and Development (OECD) have recognised the government involvement in the longevity bond market (Antolin & Blommestein, 2007).

Once the market for longevity bonds has matured, producing stable and reliable price points in the age range of 65–90, the capital markets can take over the responsibility of providing hedging capacity for this age range. The government may need to consider providing a continuous supply of deferred tail longevity bonds with payment starting at 90 (Blake et al., 2010).

Private sector organisations can issue longevity bonds. The literature suggested that pharmaceutical companies would be the natural issuers since they have a longevity supply. The longer people live, the more they shall spend on medicines. Even though this theory might be correct, Blake et al. (2010) believed that the scaling demand for longevity bonds far exceeds the conceivable supply from such companies.

However, this study found that the Malaysian government has the best potential to issue this kind of bond. The Malaysian government bonds—Malaysian Government Securities (MGS) and Government Investment Issuance (GII) bonds are issued by the Central Bank of Malaysia on behalf of the Malaysian government. Hence, the government is the best party to issue such bonds.

Figure 6.3 shows that the Malaysian government has raised the debt via bond issuance due to the requirement. In terms of percentage, the government bond issuance has maintained at 50 –60% for the past seven years. However, the trend declined from early 2013 to 2019, decreasing to 52.05% in December 2019. The Malaysian government can hedge this risk by issuing other types of bonds regarding the outstanding amount. The outstanding bond volume by the Malaysian government has proven that the Malaysian government is the best party to issue this kind of bond.

Annuity Provider or Pension Provider

As the government-linked investment company (GLIC), KWAP is one of the three main bodies that manage the pension schemes in Malaysia besides EPF and LTAT. KWAP took over the Public Services Department (PSD) Post-Pension Services Division functions in 2015. It manages the payment of pensions, gratuities, and other benefits provided under the merged fund (KWAP, 2017).

The incorporation of KWAP enables all powers, functions, activities, assets, and liabilities of the Pensions Trust Fund to be taken over by KWAP. KWAP's mission is to manage the fund (the fund) established under Sect. 6.3 of the Retirement Fund Act 2007 (Act 662). It aims

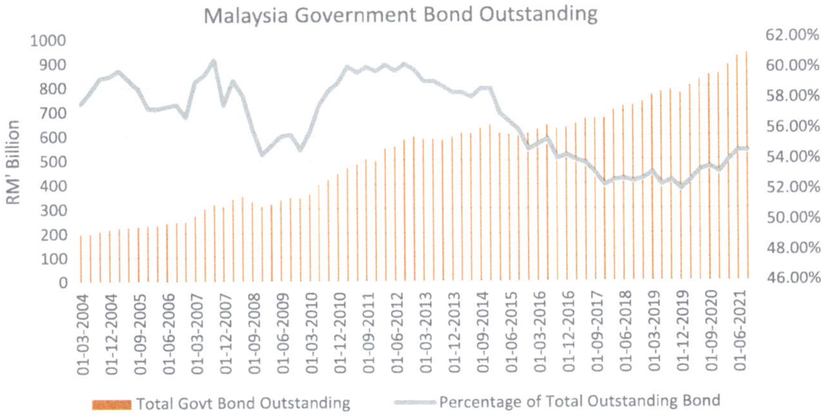

Fig. 6.3 The Malaysian government bond outstanding by quarter (2004–2021) (*Source* Bloomberg, ASEAN Development Bank)

to achieve maximised returns via benchmarking, a dynamic investment framework, and sound risk management. The fund shall assist the Federal government in financing its pension liability.

KWAP has full responsibility for investing and managing the respective fund. KWAP shall follow policies set by the investment panel and approved by the board for any new investments. The situation includes a strategic asset allocation, which needs to be reviewed periodically to ensure optimal returns from the relatively low-risk investments.

The investment policy and guidelines shall be the document that governs KWAP's investment activities. However, the status and performance of the KWAP's assets are reported monthly to the investment panel and the board. As a sole fund manager on behalf of the government, KWAP performance projection is essential to ensure the government's financial sustainability to fund the pension and future obligations.

As shown in Table 6.2, the total fund size has increased from 2007 to 2018. The fund size reached RM141 billion in 2017 before slightly declining to RM137 billion in 2018. Besides, KWAP fully adheres to the Malaysian Financial Reporting Standards (MFRS) 9 in its financial accounts in 2018, replacing the existing MFRS 139 (KWAP, 2018).

Nevertheless, despite the fund size of 137 billion in 2018, the gross and net return on investment (ROI) fell to 4.1% and 0.8%, the lowest

Table 6.2 KWAP Performance 2007–2018

Year/Element (20XX)	*07*	*08*	*09*	*10*	*11*	*12*	*13*	*14*	*15*	*16*	*17*	*18*
Fund Size (RM Billion)	48	52	62	71	79	89	100	109	118	125	141	137
Gross Investment Income (RM Billion)	3.4	2.9	3.2	4.6	4.6	5.8	6.7	6.5	6.4	6.4	9.0	7.1
Net Income (RM Billion)	3.7	0.6	5.7	4.9	4.3	5.7	6.6	4.8	4.4	4.8	8.8	1.2
Gross ROI (%)	9.2	5.9	5.6	7.1	6.3	6.8	7.1	6.2	5.4	5.4	5.8	4.1
Net ROI (%)	9.8	1.1	10	7.3	5.8	6.8	7.0	4.6	3.3	4.0	7.0	0.8

Source KWAP Financial Report

return recorded in the past 12 years. This figure raises concerns about KWAP's ability to generate enough return from its assets to meet its future obligations. Hence, it is necessary to examine whether KWAP's future pension assets can cover its liabilities.

Figure 6.4 shows the percentage of Malaysia's pension expenditure over tax revenue, which is about an average of 10.8%. The highest rate was reported at 27% in August 2020. The increasing trend in tax revenue is worrying for Malaysian policymakers. There is no more room for the Malaysian government to accept a higher pension cost in the future.

The Investors

Despite these compelling properties of longevity bonds, the market has remained stagnant. Various variables have played a role in the slow expansion of longevity bonds; these factors apply to buyers and sellers. The market is generally short on investors willing to take on longevity risk. Therefore, capital must be enticed by attractive risk-adjusted returns (Thomsen et al., 2007).

Furthermore, some externalities may obstruct market development. A component like remarkable volume is often necessary for a market to flourish. However, growth can be rapid once the volume has reached a crucial threshold. One variable contributing to the volume growth is the number of potential investors buying longevity bonds. As suggested in the literature, the lack of demand is one of the main reasons the longevity bond has failed.

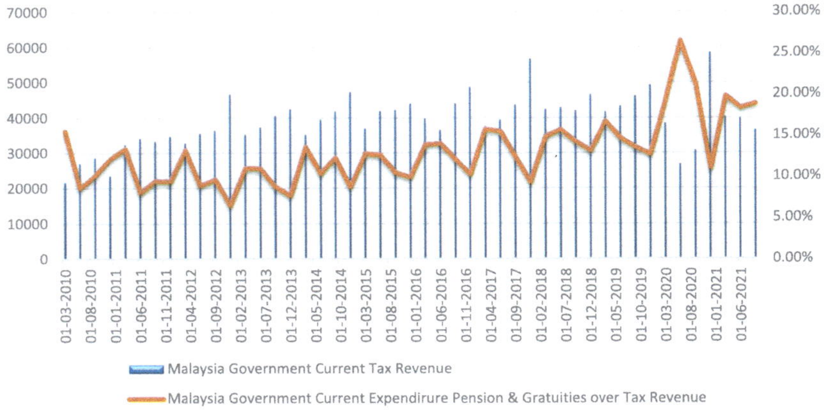

Fig. 6.4 Percentage of pension expenditure over tax revenue (*Source* Bloomberg, Bank Negara Malaysia [BNM])

Bond buyers or investors are the parties interested in investing in longevity-linked securities. The Malaysian capital market has a different landscape, supported by the government-linked investment companies (GLIC) for any government issuance or policy. Also, foreign entities are interested in investing in the Malaysian capital market. Figure 6.5 shows the number of foreign holdings in Malaysia Debt Securities. The increasing trend provides evidence that Malaysia's capital market has been trusted to be invested in.

From the investor's perspective, they have had to accept that they were buying or looking for an instrument that could prove practically possible to resell in the secondary market. Since a longevity bond is not a straight bond instrument with 25 years or more maturities, these features have it difficult to be sold as products that combine complexity and long maturities (Thomsen et al., 2007). At the same time, it has been challenging to agree on some standardisation measures, including estimating the future development in life expectancy and the related uncertainty. The lack of liquidity for this kind of bond has led investors to demand a higher liquidity premium.

The annuity provider in Malaysia's Defined Benefit pension scheme refers to KWAP, as KWAP will take over the government's responsibilities in paying the pension obligations. Hence, KWAP is the party that is

Fig. 6.5 Malaysia debt securities foreign holding (*Source* Bloomberg, Bank Negara Malaysia [BNM])

exposed to longevity risk. Figure 6.6 illustrates the proposed Malaysia's first longevity bond workflow. A new Special Vehicle Purpose (SPV) will be created to issue longevity bonds on behalf of the Malaysian government. Malaysia Pension Department under SPA will be a reference for the issuance.

Mortality Rate

Seeing how a longevity bond can hedge aggregate longevity risk requires quantifying and identifying where longevity bond is concentrated in Malaysia. Figure 6.7 shows the number of survivors out of the cohort of males aged 55 and above in Malaysia, according to age group at the end of 2020. Uncertainty is lower for younger people, and one can be confident that about 75% of males aged 55 will live for 15 years up to 70. Uncertainty increases, and it is the highest at 80 and beyond. It is estimated that 45–55% of them will survive to 85 years old and above, a considerable range. This range is known as tail risk. It is the possibility that a cohort member may survive beyond 85 years of age.

Figure 6.7 also shows the so-called tail risk, the probability that some cohort members will live beyond 85 years old.

Some claim that the government is not the natural issuer of longevity bonds because of its huge exposure to longevity risk through the social

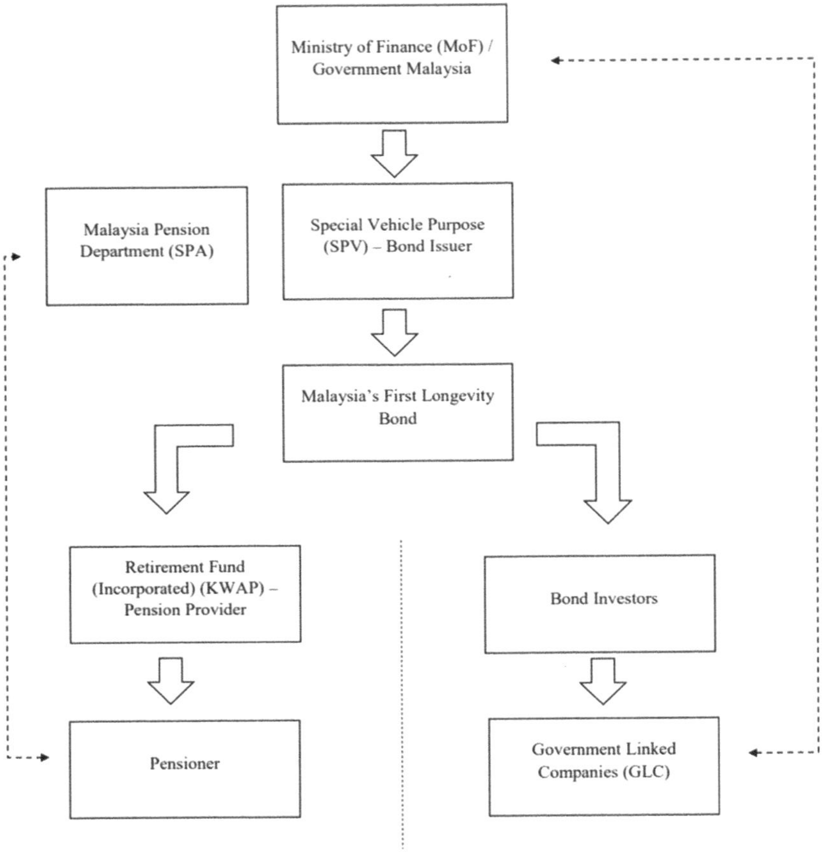

Fig. 6.6 Workflow of the proposed Malaysia's first longevity bond

security system and pensions for civil servants. Therefore, several aspects shall be considered.

First, the government would receive a longevity risk premium by issuing the bonds—the issuance would generate revenue. Second, the government can control the ultimate pension cost by increasing the official retirement age if longevity rises dramatically. Third, issuing longevity bonds shall result in a more efficient annuity market and, hence, higher

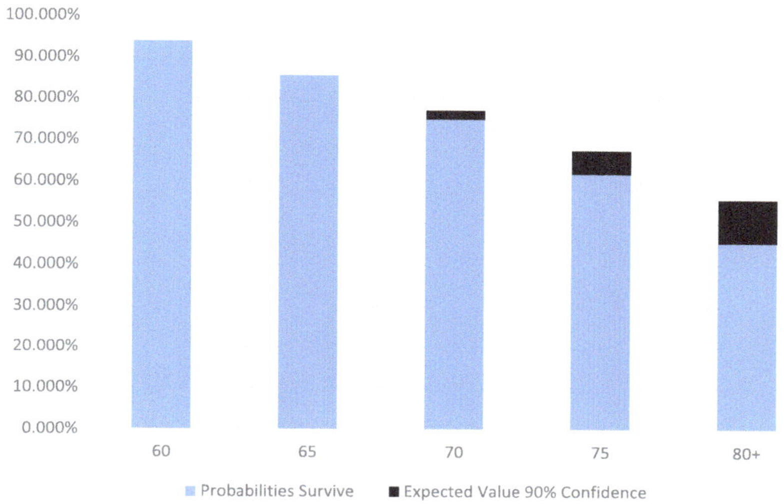

Fig. 6.7 Percentage of surviving males aged 55 and above according to a given age (*Source* Author's calculation based on the Life Abridged life table by sex and age, Malaysia, 2020)

retirement incomes, perhaps reducing the need for means-tested retirement benefits. Fourth, the total issuance shall be small concerning the overall government bond market size. Finally, the risk is consistent with the government's role in preparing a foundation for intergenerational risk-sharing.

Meanwhile, Fig. 6.8 shows projections of the number of survivors out of the cohort of females aged 55 and above in Malaysia, according to age group at the end of 2020. The areas at the top of each bar (the black portion) indicate a 90% confidence interval. Uncertainty is low for those of younger ages, and one can be confident that 79 –80% of females aged 55 will survive for 20 years up to 75. Uncertainty increases once their age increases, reaching its peak at 80 and beyond. It is estimated that 63 –71% will survive above 80. A large range-tail risk is that a cohort member may survive beyond 85 years old.

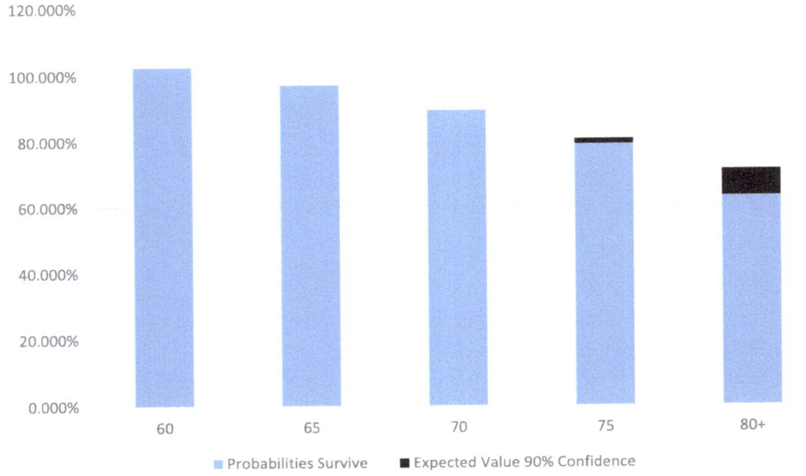

Fig. 6.8 Percentage of surviving females aged 55 according to a given age (*Source* Author's Calculation based on the Life Abridged life table by sex and age, Malaysia, 2020)

Cash Flow for the Simulation Malaysia Longevity Bond 2020

The longevity bond cash flow has been designed based on the differences between life expectancy and expectancy of life expectancy. The positive percentage indicated that the number of survivors at a given age X by DOSM is more than WHO predicted. At the same time, the negative percentage indicates that the number of survivors reported by the DOSM is less than that reported by the WHO. Figure 6.9 shows the percentage differences between the number of survivors at a given age X from the Department of Statistics Malaysia (DOSM) and the World Health Organisation (WHO).

The discrepancies between life survivors given at X between the two sources have been wider throughout the age. The data has shown how the longevity bond is practical or applicable in hedging the longevity risk after retirement. The longevity bond is issued on every cohort of 40 years old, assumed after ten years in the civil services to be eligible for the pension benefit. The longevity bond should be issued at 40 years old for every cohort. As expected, this cohort will be pensioned at 60 (20 years after in-service).

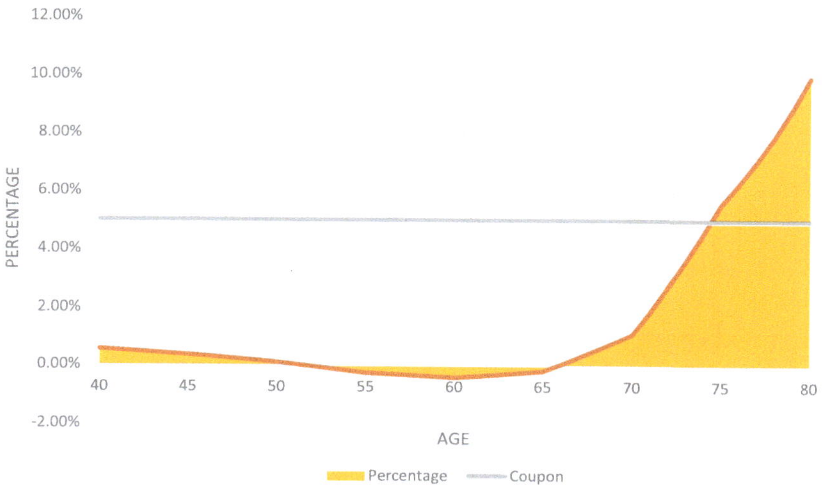

Fig. 6.9 Percentage differences between WHO and DOSM for survival at X for 2020 (*Source* Author's Calculation based on the Life Abridged life table by sex and age, Malaysia, 2020 and World Health Organisation, 2020)

The cash flow for the longevity bond is paid based on the discrepancies between the expected life survivors and real-life survivors. Based on the percentage differences between life survivors, the cash flow is presented in Table 6.3.

Table 6.3 shows that for every longevity bond issuance, the annuity provider will benefit later for every cohort. At the age of 40 to 51 years old, the coupon payment will be shared between the annuity provider (KWAP) and investors since the life expectancy is still under the coupon payment. However, the real-life survivor is less than what is expected to be in those aged 52 years old to 65 years old. At this stage, the annuity provider will not receive any coupon payment. In contrast, the investor will receive the 100% of the coupon payment. From the age of 66 to 74 years old, the Coupon portion is still shared between the investors and the annuity provider. Lastly, at 75 and above, the annuity provider will receive 100% of the coupon payment since the difference between life expectancy is more than the coupon percentage

Figure 6.10 illustrates the summary of coupon payments between the investors and annuity providers. From the age of 40 years to 51 years

Table 6.3 Longevity bond cash flow based on simulation I

Age	*Equation*	*Annuity Provider*	*Investor*
40–51 Years Old	$0 < I_{X0+t} - E(I_{X0+t}) \leq C$	Receive the Differences between expected life expectancy and real expectancy	Investors will receive the differences between expected life expectancy and real expectancy
52–65 Years Old	$I_{X0+t} - E(I_{X0+t}) \leq 0$	Zero	Receive full longevity bond coupon
66–74 Years Old	$0 < I_{X0+t} - E(I_{X0+t}) \leq C$	Receive the Differences between expected life expectancy and real expectancy	Investors will receive the differences between expected life expectancy and real expectancy
75–80 and above Years Old	$I_{X0+t} - E(I_{X0+t}) > C$	The annuity provider will receive the coupon payment	Zero

old, the proportion allocated to the annuity provider is getting lesser. Until 52 years to 65 years old, the annuity provider receives no coupon. However, the proportion of coupons for the annuity provider keeps increasing, starting when the cohort is 66 years old up to 80 years and above. The annuity provider will receive a full coupon payment from 66 years onwards, which might help hedge the portion of the longevity risk. The yellow part in the graph represents any loss that will be reduced by the annuity provider using the longevity bond instrument.

Cash Flow for the Simulation Malaysia Longevity Bond 2015

Figure 6.11 shows the discrepancies between life survivors given at X between two sources reported in 2015 have been wider throughout the age. The data has shown how the longevity bond is practical or applicable in hedging the longevity risk after retirement. The longevity bond is issued on every cohort of 40 years old, assumed after ten years in the civil services to be eligible for the pension benefit. The longevity bond should be issued at 40 years old for every cohort. This cohort will be pensioned at 60 (20 years after services).

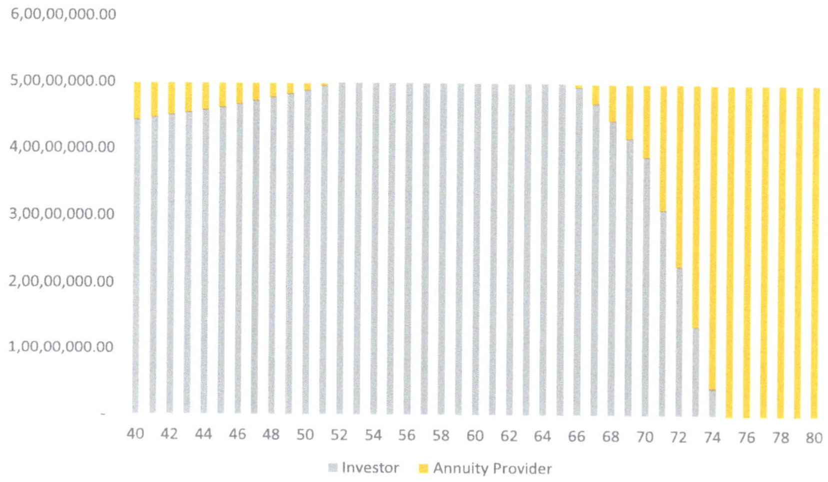

Fig. 6.10 Proportion longevity bond coupon for investors or KWAP for 2020 (*Source* Author's Calculation based on the simulation)

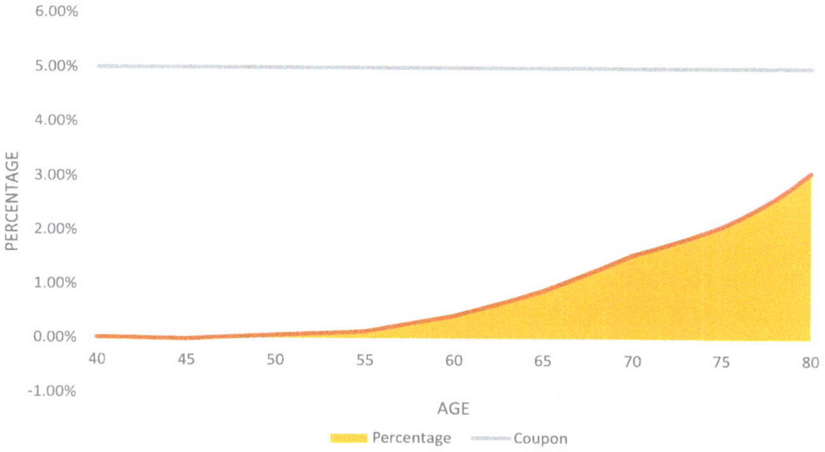

Fig. 6.11 Percentage differences between WHO and DOSM for survival at X for 2015 (*Source* Author's Calculation based on the Life Abridged life table by sex and age, Malaysia, 2015 and World Health Organisation, 2015)

Table 6.4 Longevity Bond Cash Flow based on simulation II

Age	*Equation*	*Annuity Provider*	*Investor*
40 – 80 + Years Old	$0 < I_{X0+t} - E(I_{X0+t}) \leq C$	Receive the Differences between expected life expectancy and real expectancy	The investor will receive the differences between expected life expectancy and real expectancy

The cash flow for the longevity bond for the 2015 issuance will be paid on the discrepancies between the expected life survivors and real-life survivors. Both investors and annuity providers will receive the differences between expected and real-life expectancy. Table 6.4 illustrates that the age between 40 and 80 + years old would share the coupon between annuity providers and investors.

Figure 6.12 illustrates the summary of coupon payments between the investors and annuity providers for 2015. The portion of Coupons that the investors receive gradually increases over time. The increase differs from what was reported in 2020. The annuity provider will receive a full coupon at age 67 and above. The yellow part in the graph represents any loss that will be reduced by the annuity provider using the longevity bond instrument.

Cash Flow for the Simulation Malaysia Longevity Bond 2010

Figure 6.13 shows the discrepancies between life survivors given at X between two sources reported in 2010. The discrepancies become wider throughout time. The cash flow for the longevity bond for the 2010 issuance will be paid on the differences between the expected life survivors and real-life survivors. Investors and annuity providers will receive the differences between expected and real life expectancy. Compared to 2015, 2010 reported the same pattern of Coupons. Table 6.5 illustrates that the ages between 40 years to 80 + years old will share the coupon between annuity providers and investors.

Figure 6.14 illustrates the summary of coupon payments between the investors and annuity providers for 2010. The portion of Coupons that the investors receive gradually increases over time. The pattern differs from what was reported in 2020; the annuity provider will receive a full

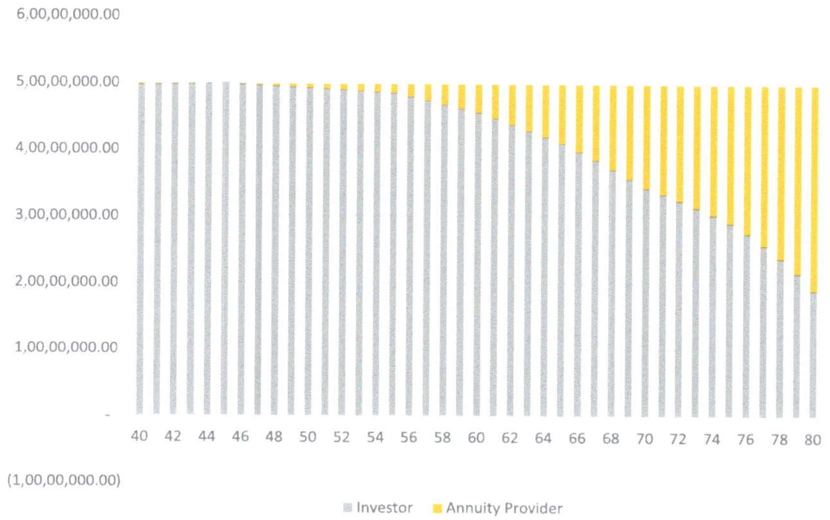

Fig. 6.12 Proportion longevity bond coupon for investors or KWAP for 2015 (*Source* Author's Calculation based on the simulation)

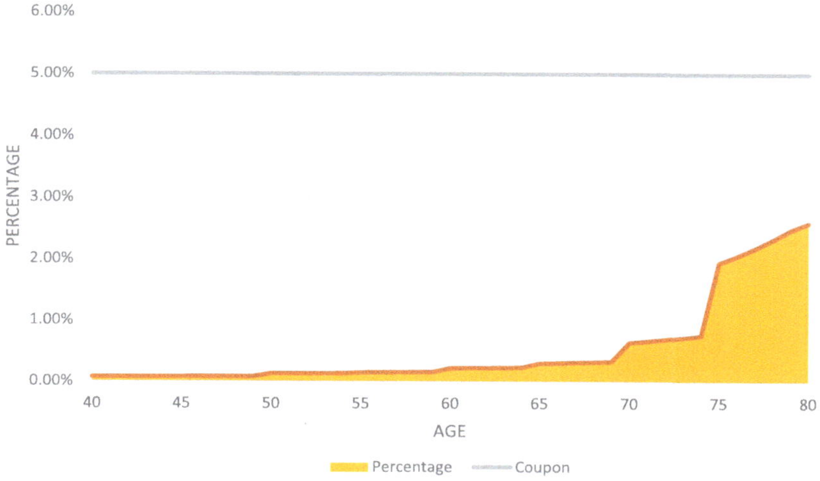

Fig. 6.13 Percentage differences between WHO and DOSM for survival at X for 2010 (*Source* Author's Calculation based on the Life Abridged life table by sex and age, Malaysia, 2010 and World Health Organisation)

Table 6.5 Longevity bond cash flow based on simulation III

Age	*Equation*	*Annuity Provider*	*Investor*
40–80 + Years Old	$0 < I_{X0+t} - E(I_{X0+t}) \leq C$	Receive the Differences between expected life expectancy and real expectancy	Investors will receive the differences between expected life expectancy and real expectancy

Coupon at age 67 and above. The yellow part in the graph represents any loss that will be reduced by the annuity provider using the longevity bond instrument. The annuity providers would be less than in 2015 and 2020.

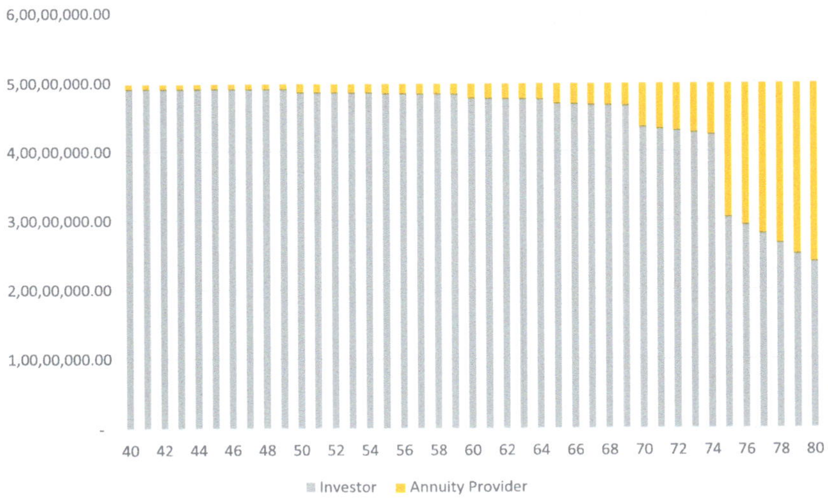

Fig. 6.14 Proportion longevity bond coupon for investors or KWAP for 2010 (*Source* Author's Calculation based on the simulation)

Summary for 2020, 2015, 2010

These three years have captured the longevity risk posed to annuity providers, showing that the number of survivors has increased from what was expected. The pattern indicates that the longevity risk would become a significant factor that needs to be addressed by the pension provider.

Introducing a longevity bond might be helpful; the late introduction of this product to the capital market might cause the annuity provider to have a loss. The Malaysian government will be beneficial at a later age when the longevity bond might help hedge the longevity risks. This study proposes that the longevity bond is an instrument where it is possible to evade the longevity risk where it impacts the pension's sustainability for the long term. Figure 6.7 demonstrates the cash flows of the longevity bond. The bond shall enable full hedging of longevity risk and allow investors to take the longevity swap market to avoid assuming the tail longevity risk, which they have no appetite for.

Introducing a longevity bond in Malaysia's capital market helps the annuity provider reduce pensioners' lives longer than expected. The longevity bond coupon covers every life that lives longer than it should be. It might not hedge 100% of the risk, but it reduces the loss the annuity provider will cover. The loss that is supposed to be covered by the annuity provider will be less in defining the longevity of people. The loss will be reduced, represented by the reduction of yellow colour.

Pricing considerations

Ultimately, the demand for longevity bonds shall depend on their price. The government would charge a risk premium—the price at which the government shall sell the bond that would exceed the expected present value of the coupons payable on the bond, discounted by the interest rate on the government securities of comparable maturities.

The bonds must also be priced to attract sponsors of the defined benefit plans that do not meet solvency capital requirements. This requirement is necessary for insurance companies holding longevity bonds to keep less capital against the risk of mortality improvements, which can be more rapid than expected. Also, other investors, including investment banks, would be discouraged from purchasing such bonds if they believe the longevity risk premium is more excessive than it should be. The Malaysian government needs to consider applying the longevity bond in transferring the risk that the KWAP could bear as a pensioner provider to the capital market.

6.10 Conclusion

Due to higher life expectancy, the Malaysian government would have significant problems sustaining a defined benefit pension plan for civil servants. In general, the Malaysian government must handle rising life expectancy through increasing revenue, reserve, and tax collection to sustain pension schemes in longer retirement age. Capital provisions have been made to serve as a general buffer against future changes in the value of pension commitment. Besides that, pension providers are still required to manage the risk to their capacity, given the uncertainty surrounding forecasts of the future development in life expectancy.

The pension industry has highlighted the tools for explicit risk management variables, such as longevity risk in managing uncertainty. Since the market has always risen and gone down, the players shall be more flexible in adopting investment strategies to bring down the cost to the pension provider. It is vital for the parties involved to leverage the market movement. In the twenty-first century, longevity bonds will be a crucial new asset class. However, the existing literature has highlighted that the insurance and reinsurance business does not have enough capital to deal with the global longevity risk. Hence, capital markets are recommended to be more efficient than the insurance industry to reduce information inconsistencies and facilitate price determination.

A life market is where longevity products have been traded. The life market assets have first-order risks uncorrelated with the traditional financial assets such as bond and equity markets, making them appealing for investors to diversify their assets portfolio. Nevertheless, this asset is still far-reaching to develop into a fully mature global capital market. Investors would also have access to a new asset class whose return is unrelated to more established asset classes like bonds, stocks, and real estate.

Hence, this chapter answers the viability and practicality of adopting the longevity bond in Malaysia to lower the longevity risk due to concerns regarding the defined benefit pension system for public employees. The result of this study proposes that the Malaysian government needs to hedge the longevity risk. Malaysia's population projection in 2020 provides statistical evidence of tail risk in the Malaysian population necessary for the tail risk concerning longevity index bond. The three-year simulation results show that the applicable longevity bonds coupon will benefit the annuity provider after age 67. Simultaneously, the suggested longevity bond coupon rate should be increased over time to capture the longevity risk premium in the long run.

The capacity to hedge aggregate longevity risk and the existence of a market price for longevity risk will benefit numerous parties. This study suggests that the Malaysian government is the best party to issue longevity bonds as the proposed structures. Hence, the Malaysian government would gain by reducing borrowing since longevity investors would be willing to accept lower returns than the lower cost for the Malaysian government.

References

Antolin, P., & Blommestein, H. (2007). Governments and the market for longevity-indexed bonds. *OECD Working Papers on Insurance and Private Pensions*, *4*. https://doi.org/10.1787/260561411283

Blake, D., Cairns, A. J. G., Dowd, K., & Kessler, A. R. (2019). Still living with mortality: The longevity risk transfer market after one decade. *British Actuarial Journal, 24*, 1–20. https://doi.org/10.1017/S1357321718000259

Blake, D. (2018). Longevity: A new asset class. *Journal of Asset Management, 19*(5), 278–300. https://doi.org/10.1057/s41260-018-0084-9

Blake, D., Boardman, T., & Cairns, A. (2010). The case for longevity bonds. *Center for Retirement Research, Boston College, 10*.

Blake, D., Boardman, T., & Cairns, A. (2014). Sharing longevity risk: Why governments should issue longevity bonds. *North American Actuarial Journal, 18*(1), 258–277. https://doi.org/10.1080/10920277.2014.883229

Blake, D., Brockett, P., Cox, S., & MacMinn, R. (2011). Longevity Risk and Capital Markets: The 2009–2010 Update. *North American Actuarial Journal, 15*(2), 141–149. https://doi.org/10.1080/10920277.2011.10597614

Blake, D., & Burrows, W. (2007). Survivor bonds: Helping to hedge mortality risk. *Journal Risk and Insurance, 68*(2), 339. https://doi.org/10.2307/2678106

Blommestein, H. J. (2006). Factors for a successful market in longevity-indexed government bonds: A public debt management perspective. *Pensions: An*

International Journal, *11*(2), 113–119. https://doi.org/10.1057/palgrave.pm.5940012

Cairns, A. J. G., Blake, D., & Dowd, K. (2008). Modelling and Management of Mortality Risk: A review. *Scandinavian Actuarial Journal*, 2–3, 79–113. https://doi.org/10.1080/03461230802173608

Cairns, A. J. G. (2013). Robust hedging of longevity risk. *Journal of Risk and Insurance*, *80*(3), 621–648. https://doi.org/10.1111/j.1539-6975.2013.01525.x

Chuang, S. L., & Brockett, P. L. (2014). Modeling and pricing longevity derivatives using stochastic mortality rates and the esscher transform. *North American Actuarial Journal*, *18*(1), 22–37. https://doi.org/10.1080/10920277.2013.873708

Coughlan, G. D., Khalaf-allah, M., Ye, Y., Kumar, S., Cairns, A. J. G., Blake, D., Dowd, K., & Row, B. (2010). *Longevity Hedging 101. 73*(4), 647–672.

Hussein, N. (2019). The Malaysian pension system. *Nomura Foundation*, 15–20. http://www.nomurafoundation.or.jp/en/wordpress/wp-content/uploads/2019/03/NJACM3-2SP19-04.pdf

KWAP. (2017). KWAP Annual Report 2017. *KWAP Website*. https://www.kwap.gov.my/EN/UsefulInformation/Publication/AnnualReports/KWAPAnnualReport2017.pdf

KWAP. (2018). KWAP Annual Report 2018. *KWAP Website*, *86*(3), 64–65. https://www.kwap.gov.my/EN/UsefulInformation/Publication/AnnualReports/KWAPAnnualReport2018.pdf

Li, J. S. H., & Hardy, M. R. (2012). Measuring basis risk in longevity hedges. *North American Actuarial Journal*, *15*(2), 177–200. https://doi.org/10.1080/10920277.2011.10597616

Li, J., Tan, C. I., Tang, S., & Liu, J. (2019). On the optimal hedge ratio in index-based longevity risk hedging. *European Actuarial Journal*, *9*(2), 445–461. https://doi.org/10.1007/s13385-019-00199-w

Lin, Y., & Cox, S. H. (2005). *Securitisation of Mortality Risks in Life Annuities.*, *72*(2), 227–252.

Liu, Y., & Li, J. S. H. (2018). A strategy for hedging risks associated with period and cohort effects using Q-Forwards. *Insurance: Mathematics and Economics*, *78*, 267–285. https://doi.org/10.1016/j.insmatheco.2017.09.007

Rappaport, A. M., & Parikh, A. (2002). Living to 100 and beyond: Implications of longer life spans. *North American Actuarial Journal*, *6*(3), 45–53. https://doi.org/10.1080/10920277.2002.10596056

Richards, S., & Gavin, J. (2004, October 26). *Financial aspects of longevity risk, The Staple Inn Actuarial Society.*

Thomsen, G. J., Andersen, J. V., & Markets, F. (2007). Longevity bonds—a financial market instrument to manage longevity risk. *Society*, *27*(27), 29–44.

WHO. (2020). *Life Tables by Country - Malaysia*. Mortality and Global Health Estimates. https://apps.who.int/gho/data/view.main.60090?lang=en

Yang, S. S., Huang, H. C., & Yeh, Y. Y. (2019). Optimal longevity hedging framework for insurance companies considering basis and mispricing risks. *Journal of Risk and Insurance, 86*(3), 783–805. https://doi.org/10.1111/jori.12238

Yew, S. Y., & Cheong, K. C. (2013). Ageing and the economic welfare of Southeast Asian Nations. *Malaysian Journal of Economic Studies, 50*(2), 101–106.

CHAPTER 7

Current State and the Way Forward

7.1 A Comparison to Defined Contribution Pension Scheme

Most of the studies done on the Malaysian pension scheme have focused on the Employment Provident Fund (EPF). The EPF-based pension scheme is a Defined Contribution (DC) pension scheme. Kuhlmann and Nullmeier (2022) review two different types of contribution-based pension systems: pension systems that largely follow a Bismarckian logic and pension systems that largely rely on national provident funds. The Malaysian EPF, being the latter, is a national provident fund. It satisfies a number of criteria as outlined by Kaseke et al. (2011). Provident funds are the legacy of the British colonial rule. The funds have the following characteristics:

a. They are compulsory for those in the formal employment with larger employers;
b. They operate as defined contribution schemes managed as part of the public sector;
c. Both employees and employers pay contributions;
d. By design, they accumulate interest based on defined rates;
e. Instead of regular payments, most provident funds rely on lump sum payments for employees who enter retirement age Kaseke et al. (2011).

M. I. Abdul Rahman and W. Y. Lau, *Pension at Stake*,
https://doi.org/10.1007/978-981-97-2324-9_7

7.2 A Comparison to Defined Benefit Pension Scheme

In contrast, a pension scheme aims to provide future economic security to retirees and their survivors after retiring and in the event of death. The government offers a Defined Benefit (DB) pension scheme for pensionable civil servants. As a result of the rapidly rising pattern of pension costs for public servants in Malaysia, the long-term sustainability of the pension scheme has become an issue of debate.

As discussed in earlier chapters, the public pension scheme is entrusted to KWAP. One of the main features of the managed pension fund is that the fund managers can pool investment risk across individuals and spread risk over a long tenure. KWAP, one of Malaysia's primary pension providers, has strategies for managing an optimal asset allocation to maximise the return. Within 13 years, from 2007 to 2020, KWAP managed to have a positive ROI throughout these years. However, the results have shown that KWAP's performance has deteriorated since 2007. This trend is because the additional risk-taking by KWAP is not reflected by the additional alpha return as measured by the ROI.

A comprehensive risk management strategy is already in place to reduce any potential negative consequences on its performance. KWAP has another big room to invest efficiently using Capital Market Line (CML) and Efficient Frontier as a baseline. The result shows that KWAP should reduce fixed-income allocation and start having more international exposures or stocks. The money market seems surprisingly a safe asset allocation with the lowest risk exposure. However, it provides a steady return to the funds. Hence, increased allocation in the money market is the answer. The strategy will sustain this organisation to meet its future commitment.

7.3 A Means to an End

The three main pension schemes are the defined benefit pension scheme for civil servants and defined contribution schemes for EPF and LTAT. The post-retirement period is crucial for the elderly to survive comfortably. In terms of the civil service pension scheme, the Malaysian government needs to balance economic sustainability against the well-being of pensioners. The Civil Service pension scheme needs re-evaluation and restructuring to ensure long-term sustainability. The government must have the political will to revamp the public sector pension scheme for long-term solvency and self-sustainability. Such a move would absolve the government from shouldering the burden of pension liabilities, which have increased over the years. The first step to securing a viable self-funded system that can provide the benefits promised to exist or future retirees is radical reform of the public sector pension programme.

The long-term financial viability of Malaysia's pension system is threatened by several factors, which highlights the need for change. Among them are the shifting demographics, the rise in pension recipients, the expansion of pension coverage, and the rising cost of pensions. Additional issues include the institutional ability to support reform and sustain the pension scheme in the long term. Hence, civil service pension system reforms are required when costs are growing and revenues and investment income are insufficient in the long run.

7.4 Summary of Findings

The findings from this book demonstrate the need for Malaysia's government to revamp the public sector pension scheme for long-term sustainability. First, the regression results show that the determinants of Malaysian pension costs are emolument, life expectancy, Malaysian population over 65, and the number of pensioners. At the same time, in the future, life expectancy will also pose a longevity risk for the government's fiscal space. It is also discovered that the ratio of pension cost to OPEX will reduce if the size of the Malaysian economy is enlarged. Therefore, the economy should be further enhanced by the expanding number of civil servants. Additionally, expanding Gross National Product (GNP) could be an alternative perspective to ensure that the national growth rate exceeds the growth rate of public servants for the long-term sustainability of the Malaysian pension scheme.

Secondly, although the KWAP's fund size has increased over the years, the forecast numbers show that the KWAP pension-funded ratio will range from 0.43 to 0.50 from 2021 to 2030. Hence, the fund will be underfunded by a cumulative amount of RM135 billion (nominal value) from 2021 to 2030. The ten-year projection from 2020 to 2030 suggests that the funded ratio will remain below 0.50, implying that Malaysian retirement funds will remain underfunded over the long run. Hence, despite not having a full federal mandate yet to cover Malaysia's pension liabilities, KWAP requires more funding from the Malaysian government.

Regarding asset allocation strategy, the results indicate that KWAP remains conservative in managing pension funds. It is recommended that KWAP reduces fixed-income allocation and increases international exposures or stocks. The money market seems surprisingly a safe asset allocation strategy, with the lowest risk exposure but a steady return on the funds. Hence, increasing the money market allocation could be a possible solution to sustain the Malaysian pension scheme. However, a higher proportion of ESG-rated securities by KWAP has benefited the portfolio. Since the result has shown that ESG-rated stocks provide a higher return and lower risk than non-rated ESG stocks, this might help them grow the portfolio bigger. Moreover, this study also found that ESG-rated securities provide a higher return per unit of risk relative to non-ESG-rated stocks. As a policy implication, the ESG-rated investment has impacted the pension fund by delivering higher returns and lower risk.

Thirdly, this study demonstrated that the minimum years of service required for pension eligibility should be increased to at least 20 years. The current minimum service requirement of ten (10) years is unsustainable, as pension funds will need a higher required rate of 50% to sustain the pension benefit. Simultaneously, the Malaysian government should increase the contribution rate to 13% and above per worker to KWAP. Despite literature suggesting extending the retirement age, this study found that raising the retirement age from 55 to 60 does not result in a reduction in pension expense as there are no significant changes in the required return. Moreover, there is a need for the government to set a minimum funding ratio for the KWAP pension fund to endure the scheme's long-term sustainability (Abdul Rahman& Lau, 2023; Irfan & Lau, 2023, 2024).

Fourthly, this study proposed a new flow of the longevity bond issued in the Malaysian Capital market. The result proves that the Malaysian government is the best party to issue the longevity bond as the capacity to absorb the liquidity volume is high via a new Special Purpose Vehicle (SPV). Malaysia's population projection in 2020 proves statistical evidence of tail risk in the Malaysian population necessary for the longevity bond requirement. Based on the simulation for three years in five gaps (2020, 2015, and 2010), the results have shown that the applicable longevity bonds coupon will benefit the annuity provider after the age of 67 years old onwards. Simultaneously, the suggested longevity bond coupon rate should be increased over time to capture the longevity risk premium in the long run.

7.5 Current State and Lessons Drawn

Jaafar et al. (2018) argue that there is a need to reform the existing pension schemes in Malaysia. They argue that demographic challenges such as increased life expectancy, falling fertility rate, and population ageing will pose a risk to pension schemes in Malaysia. In designing a good pension scheme, one needs to examine the issue of pension coverage, pension benefit adequacy, and also family structure (Suhaimi & Mansor, 2013).

7.6 Suggestions and the Way Forward

The research outcome of this study is purely based on the secondary data pulled from multiple sources. All results, conclusions, and recommendations are influenced by the timing factor when the data are retrieved. Hence, a different outcome and recommendation might be drawn if the data are retrieved at other times. This study could be extended by exploring derivatives gratuities or other names for the extension benefit. Future research may include the derivative gratuity in the retirement fund calculation and analysis. Is there a way to substitute the current defined benefit pension scheme with other kinds of pension schemes? Below are the two options to replace the current defined benefit pension civil pension scheme:

First, looking at the examples from other quasi-government institutions, the defined contribution schemes with higher contribution ratios from the public sector employers relative to the lower contribution ratios from the civil servants seem to be a viable option as a transitory measure to replace the defined benefit pension scheme.

Second, Jaafar et al. (2018) suggest a systematic reform is needed, such as shifting the unfunded defined benefit (DB) scheme to a funded defined contribution (DC) scheme. Citing the study by Brook (2007), more than 25 governments around the world have implemented some form of market-oriented reform or "privatisation". This kind of shift will increase domestic savings, enhance the development of the national capital market, and lead to higher economic growth (Hviding & Merette, 1998; World Bank, 1994).

Retirement planning is not the sole responsibility of the government. Hence, some scholars, Pak and Estrada (2012) suggest a few lessons for developing economies, such as the introduction of multi-pillar pension benefits, an increase in the retirement age for formal and private sector labour force, an increase in awareness of financial literacy and financial knowledge, and all retirement benefits must be turned into pension annuity, so that the pensioners will continue to receive a stream of monthly benefits in their post-retirement period.

References

Abdul Rahman, M. I., & Lau, W.Y. (2023). Is the KWAP defined benefit pension fund sustainable in the long run? *International Journal of Banking and Finance, 18*(2), 97–126. https://doi.org/10.32890/ijbf2023.18.2.5

Brook, S. M. (2007). Globalisation and pension reform in Latin America. *Latin America Political and Society, 49*(4), 31–62.

Hviding, K., & Merette, M. (1998). *Macroeconomic effects of pension reforms in the context of ageing populations: Overlapping generations model simulations for seven OECD countries*. Head of Publications Service, OECD.

Irfan, M., & Lau, W-Y. (2023). Determinants of pension fund's required return: A scenario-based simulation of civil service pension fund, *Australasian Accounting, Business and Finance Journal, 17*(4), 2023, 100–127. https://doi.org/10.14453/aabfj.v17i4.07

Irfan, M., & Lau, W.-Y. (2024). Asset allocation and performance of Malaysian civil service pension fund, *Australasian Accounting, Business and Finance Journal, 18*(1), 86–107. https://doi.org/10.14453/aabfj.v18i1.06

Jaafar, R., Daly, K., & Mishra, A. (2019). Challenges facing Malaysia pension scheme in an era of ageing population. *Finance Research Letters, 30*, 334–340.

Kaseke, E., Midgley, J., & Piachaud, D. (2011). The British Influence on Social Security Policy: Provident Funds in Asia and Africa. In J. Midgley & D. Piachaud (Eds.), *Colonialism and welfare: Social policy and the British imperial legacy* (pp. 144–158). Edward Elgar Publishing.

Kuhlmann, J., & Nullmeier, F. (2022). Causal mechanisms in the development of contribution-based pension systems in South Korea, Vietnam, Sri Lanka, and Malaysia. In J. Kuhlmann, & F. Nullmeier (Eds.), *Causal mechanisms in the global development of social policies. Global dynamics of social policy*. Palgrave Macmillan. https://doi.org/10.1007/978-3-030-91088-4_3

Park, D., & Estrada, G. B. (2012). *Developing Asia's Pension System and Old-age Income Support*. ADBI Working Paper Series, April 2012(358), 1–32.

Suhaimi, A. S., & Mansor, N. (2013). Population ageing and social protection in Malaysia. *Malaysian Journal of Economic Studies, 50*(2), 139–156.

World Bank. (1994). *Averting the old age crisis: Policies to protect the old and promote growth*. Retrieved from Washington, D.C.: World Bank Group. http://documents.worldbank.org/curated/en/973571468174557899/Averting-the-old-age-crisis-policies-to-protect-the-old-and-promote-growth

Index

M. I. Abdul Rahman and W. Y. Lau, *Pension at Stake*,
https://doi.org/10.1007/978-981-97-2324-9

The manufacturer's authorised representative in the EU is Springer Nature Customer Service Centre GmbH, Europaplatz 3, 69115 Heidelberg, Germany. If you have any concerns regarding our products, please contact ProductSafety@springernature.com

Printed and bound by CPI Group (UK) Ltd, Croydon, CR0 4YY
01/10/2026
02225931-0001